MORE AMAZING STORIES
of Divine Intervention

MORE AMAZING STORIES
of Divine Intervention

JAMES L. ("LEE") LAMBERT

XULON ELITE

Xulon Press Elite
2301 Lucien Way #415
Maitland, FL 32751
407.339.4217
www.xulonpress.com

Paperback ISBN-13: 978-1-66285-949-6
Ebook ISBN-13: 978-1-66285-950-2

Table of Contents

Chapter 1

Ike's Commitment To God And Our Nation

On October 14, 1890 Dwight (Ike) David Eisenhower was born in Denison, Texas. His parents were David J. and Elizabeth Eisenhower. Dwight was the third of seven sons. David and Elizabeth moved their family to Abliene, Kansas in 1892. There, Dwight's father worked as a railroad mechanic and later for a creamery store.

As a young boy Dwight was raised in a devote Christian home where they attended a small Anabaptist denomination church. (1) However, Dwight at that time was more interested in reading his mother's military history books than other themed books. Dwight graduated from the local high school in 1909.

During the next year the young man worked part time at the local fire department as well as the local creamery store where his father was employed. At the urging of a friend, Dwight applied for enrollment at the United States Military Academy at West Point, and entered an entrance exam competition. Dwight, as one of the winners of the contest, was accepted into the Academy.

Dwight attended West Point from the fall of 1911 to his graduation in 1915. Due to the mandatory service obligation required of the school's graduating students, Dwight was now prepared to serve as an officer in the military.

By the fall of 1915 Dwight Eisenhower was assigned to serve in the U.S. Army as a second lieutenant in San Antonio, Texas. It was there where he ultimately met and married his future wife, Mamie Doud.

During the next 10 years it became apparent to Dwight's superiors that the young man excelled in his ability to lead and encourage those under his command. Dwight and Mamie had to frequently relocate due to the variety of assignments and promotions Dwight received in the military. It was around this time period when Dwight and his wife Mamie lived on or near military bases in five different states from Texas to New Jersey.

Sadly, it was also during this time when their first son, Doud, who was born in 1921, died of Scarlet Fever at the age of three. John, his brother, had been born two years earlier.

In 1924 Dwight made arrangements to attend the Army's graduate school in Leavenworth, Kansas. He intensified his study of battlefield strategy which included military strategies which were used by the allied forces during World War I. Ultimately, studying battlefields was a good preparation for Ike's later role in directing the Western Front during World War ll. By 1926, Dwight graduated first in his class. (3)

During the next ten years, Dwight Eisenhower advanced in rank, time and again. During the early 1930s Dwight "was appointed as an aid to Army Chief of Staff Douglas MacArthur who became his mentor and boss through the 1930s." (3) Both men were based in Washington, D.C.

In 1935 U.S. President Franklin Roosevelt appointed General MacArthur as military advisor to Filipino President Manuel Quezon. At that time, the Philippines were an American colony as a result of the Spanish-American War. Roosevelt was preparing the Philippines for their independence which was scheduled to take place in 1946.

It was also during this time when General MacArthur ordered Eisenhower, his chief advisor, to join him in the Philippines.

For the first time Dwight was separated from his family for a year, until Mamie and John joined him in 1936. Dwight was assigned to train the Filipino Army for their planned independence. (3)

By late 1939 Dwight learned of the German invasion of Poland. He and Mamie listened to British Prime Minister Neville Chamberlain's declaration of war against Germany and its leader, Adolf Hitler. (3) Eisenhower later commented by saying that "Hitler's record with the Jews, his rape of Austria, of the Czechs, the Slovaks and now the Poles is as bad as that of any barbarian of the Dark Ages." (3a)

Eisenhower recognized that the United States would eventually become involved in this new European war. Dwight, now a Colonel in the U.S. Army, and his family moved back to the United States in 1941.

On the morning of December 7th, 1941, Dwight was shocked along with the rest of the world with the Japanese invasion and bombing of the U.S. Naval base in Honolulu, Hawaii. A few days later (on December 12th) he was asked to appear in Chief of Staff General Marshall's office in Washington DC. General Marshall was seeking Dwight's assessment of the future of the Philippines, considering the Japanese invasion of that island had already begun four days earlier.

Dwight was forthright about his lack of confidence in the Filipino army and their ability to defend themselves and their island.(3) Since time was now of the essence, he suggested that it was better for the U.S. Naval forces to ensure that the sea lanes were kept open to the neighboring islands including Fiji, Australia, New Zealand and others. Dwight calculated that this would allow future U.S. military endeavors against the Japanese to be more successful. Eisenhower clearly understood that it would take months, if not at least a year, to prepare U.S. forces to invade a variety of islands around the South Pacific which were thousands of miles away from America's west coast.

Eisenhower became convinced that it was more important for the United States to focus on supporting our allies in Europe who were in immediate danger of being taken over by the Nazi regime. This included countries such as France, England, Norway, Sweden, Belgium and even Russia. Nazi German forces were already knocking on the door of a number of U.S. allies at that time.

In February of 1942, Dwight Eisenhower was appointed to be the Head of the War Plans Division of the U.S. military, based in Washington, DC. It was around this time when he proclaimed to U.S. Army Chief of Staff General Marshall "that the three keys to Allied strategy should be Britain's security, keeping Russia in the war and defending the Middle East."(3)

Eisenhower was convinced along with his military Chief of Staff, George Marshall that the wise move would be to attack and confront the Axis forces in Europe directly. While Dwight insisted that the U.S. and its allies would benefit more by first invading France, British Prime Minister Winston Churchill convinced U.S. President Roosevelt that the initial invasion should be to confront the Axis powers in North Africa.

Those series of battles in North Africa began on November of 1942 and would ultimately include portions of the Mediterranean coast. The Allies benefitted nevertheless, because the war in North Africa was over by May of 1943. (3)

Due to the close proximity of allied forces in Europe, it was now clear to Roosevelt and Churchill that allied troops should next attack Sicily and then Italy (an ally of Hitler's Germany) by August of '43. Again this phase of the war was costly to all but it was still an important win for the allied forces.

During this time, FDR, Churchill and Russian leader Joseph Stalin would periodically meet to discuss allied war strategy. It was deter-mined by consensus that an invasion of France should be the next move. For that campaign, President Roosevelt chose General Eisenhower to lead the invasion.

Eisenhower understood that unity among the allies was important. However Dwight was deeply grieved by the numerous letters he received from parents of soldiers who had died in battle. As the newly assigned five-star General of the allied forces, Dwight Eisenhower pri-oritized the lives of his soldiers over any objective without ultimate victory. That is why it was vital for him, as commanding General, to decide strategically where the invasion would occur.

Dwight realized the necessity to properly train his troops for this invasion which would be by sea. His troops spent the spring of 1944 doing just that. General Eisenhower also knew he had to confuse the enemy as to where the invasion would take place. He used U.S. and British war planes to bomb other parts of German occupied Europe in order to divert Axis attention.

By January 1944 Hitler was redirecting his forces to the western and eastern portions of his borders in order to defend Axis rule throughout the portions of Europe which Germany still controlled. The question now was, among Allied and Axis leaders alike, where would the location be of the next Allied invasion?

Eisenhower, along with his Allied commanders decided Normandy was the best location for the invasion. The allied commander went so far as to send air force incursions into the very northern part of France to convince German military leaders that the Allied invasion would take place at Pas de Calais. (3) Pas de Calais was located on the Atlantic coast next to Belgium. It was also the closest French territory to Britain.

With the invasion scheduled for June 5th, it was decided by General Eisenhower to delay the allied attack by one day due to weather concerns. Prior to the invasion the commanding General personally met with a large number of the troops to encourage them in this historic military endeavor.

D-Day occurred on June 6th, 1944. The invasion involved over 160,000 allied troops, 7,000 ships and 10,000 airborne planes. It commenced very early that morning with the soldiers leaving by boat from the coast of Great Britain. Clearly the airborne element of Ike's forces helped limit German reinforcements from killing thousands of the Allied troops before the beachheads were secure. (3) It would take another six weeks before the allied troops would eventually free themselves from the French coastline and advance into the heartland of France.

While the invasion was costly for the allies, it would lead Eisenhower's troops to free the French people from their Axis oppressors. Over a period of the next 11 months much would occur militarily in war torn Europe.

By August of 1944, British and Canadian troops liberated the Netherlands. As for France, allied troops reached the Seine River and liberated Marseille. On August 25, 1944 Paris, the French capital, was liberated. (3) Within the next few months Charles de Gaulle was named as the temporary head of France's government. General de Gaulle had earned the respect of Eisenhower and other allied leaders for his efforts as the leader of the French resistance against the German occupation of his homeland, France.

By late 1944 Germany counter attacked with its strongest resistance against allied troops to date with 'the Battle of the Bulge'. With the joining of the American forces, the allied troops were able to defeat the German offense though the victory was a costly one for the U.S. The combined American and British troops under Eisenhower's command reached the German border by March of 1945.

By now Stalin's Soviet army was getting close to the eastern border of the city of Berlin. Their action initiated a response from Germany's military. However, by April of '45 Allied troops had completely encircled the German capitol city. On May 2, Soviet troops captured the German Reichstag, their government's headquarters, in Berlin.

General Eisenhower had requested that the Germans surrender but it was later discovered that their leader, Adolf Hitler, was living in an under-ground bunker in Berlin. By May 7th Germany had surrendered. It was suspected that the German leader had committed suicide.

A lot had occurred during the fifteen months since Eisenhower had taken command of the allied troops in Western Europe. Dwight along with the thousands of U.S. Army, Navy and Air Force soldiers under his command had been separated from their families in America for far too long. Yet these same soldiers had delivered millions of people from Hitler's totalitarian rule in a number of countries that included France, Belgium, Sweden, Norway, the Netherlands, Denmark, Italy, and Greece. Their sacrifice was not forgotten.

It was also during this time that allied troops exposed the horrific German holocaust of Jewish men, women and children which occurred in several occupied countries. The slaughter of over 6 million Jewish people from the late 1930's to the end of the war in 1945 deeply disturbed the 55 year old general. In a letter Dwight wrote to Mamie he said: "I visited a German Internment camp. I never dreamed that such cruelty, bestiality, and savagery could really exist in this world! It was horrible." (3)

From his Bible readings as a child, Eisenhower understood the importance of the Jewish people. He knew that the Jewish people had an important role in establishing God's relationship with mankind. His mother had taught him the importance of having God in his life. However, Ike's life since he was a young man had been consumed with the military and the position he currently had in a war involving nations from across the world.

After the conclusion of the war in Europe together with the Japanese surrender on September 2, 1945, Dwight was made military governor of the U.S. occupied zone of Germany. (1) It wasn't too long before he was able to return home to his family in Abilene, Kansas. For the next five years he held a variety of positions including the U.S. Army Chief of Staff in Washington D.C., the President of Columbia University in New York City, and finally as allied commander of the NATO.(5) (1)

In early 1952, Dwight attended a NATO meeting in Paris, France. He was approached by several senior members of the Republican Party who encouraged him to run for President. It wasn't long thereafter that he would do just that. (6)

The 62 year old candidate was concerned that some prominent Democrat Party Senators and Representatives wanted the U.S. to be isolated from any future foreign engagements. The former U.S. Army

General didn't believe this was wise considering the expansion of communism around the world from the late 1940s.

Eisenhower had seen, first hand, what communism had done to countries in Eastern Europe which had come under its influence and in some cases, occupation by the Soviet Union. He was also alarmed about communist expansion into China and Korea where American troops were currently engaged in a war to keep Korea free.

On November 4, 1952 Dwight 'Ike' Eisenhower was elected President. Within two weeks of his inauguration, he not only joined the National Presbyterian Church but was the first President in history to be baptized while in office. Prior to this, President elect Eisenhower was not a member of any church. Ike made the decision to join the church at the urging of the Reverend Billy Graham. He knew that following God was especially important now during this time in his life. Rev. Graham had earlier met with the Republican candidate and encouraged him to set an example by joining a church. (7)

Dwight realized that it was essential for him as a national leader to have faith in God. On January 20, 1953 he began his inauguration address to the nation with an opening prayer that he personally wrote.

The new President soon realized during this time that communism was gaining more and more influence around the world. The communist revolution was originally initiated in 1917 by Russia's leader Vladimir Lenin. Lenin based his leadership of the Russian government on the writings of political theorist Karl Marx who was an atheist. Lenin and others in his government's leadership openly opposed the Christian faith.

Mao Tse-Tung, a committed communist dating back to 1935, was the leader of mainland China when Eisenhower took office. China's influence in southern Asia would, over time, help establish other communist governments in neighboring countries including Vietnam, Cambodia and North Korea. As the newly elected President, Eisenhower wanted to clearly establish the difference between a free, democratically run country like America and communist regimes such as China and the Soviet Union.

During his first year as President, Dwight arranged for an armistice and a peace agreement which ultimately divided Korea into two countries: one democratic to the south and one communist to the north. This ended the Korean War. By 1955 President Eisenhower would also meet with British and Soviet leaders to lessen the threat of atomic war. He believed his efforts in promoting peace and belief in God would distinguish America's freedom from communist oppression.

By now it was evident to most Americans that President Eisenhower wanted to make belief in God a hallmark of his administration. "His Cabinet meetings would begin with a moment of silent prayer. He initiated the National Prayer Breakfast, and welcomed Rev. Billy Graham into the White House as a spiritual advisor". (5)

During the next 18 months there was a concerted effort by the President to publically honor God by placing the words 'under God' into the Pledge of Allegiance. As the President was signing this legislation to add the phrase, he said "from this day forward millions of school children will daily proclaim in every city and town, every village and rural school house, the dedication of our nation and our people to the Almighty." (7) By 1956 the motto 'In God We Trust' was also placed on all printed U.S. currency. It was during that same year when Dwight Eisenhower won re-election for another term as President by an even larger margin than in 1952.

For the next four years America was to experience a period of peace and economic prosperity. It is estimated that from 1940 to 1960 church attendance also dramatically increased by approximately 20 percent. (8) It was also during this time period when Alaska and Hawaii were granted statehood into the United States.

On January 21st of 1961, Dwight and his wife Mamie retired to their farmhouse in Gettysburg, PA. It was in his office at Gettysburg College where the former President Dwight would write his memoirs and would hold periodic interviews and meetings.

It was during his retirement when Dwight became actively involved with Gettysburg's local Presbyterian Church which was pastored by James Mac Askill. In 1963, approximately two years after he left office, Ike became particularly disturbed when he found out the Supreme Court had banned Bible reading in public schools. Ike delivered a sermon at the Gettysburg Presbyterian church and stated that he could "not see how any Supreme Court in the world can declare teachings in this vein illegal"(9).

By late 1968, the former President's health declined and he was transferred to Walter Reed Hospital in Bethesda, Maryland. Dwight's old friend, Billy Graham, whom he had once called "America's Pastor" again paid him a visit. It was during this last meeting when he would again recite to Ike the plan of salvation, after which Dwight said "I'm ready." (9)

On March 28th, 1969 the 78 year old former President passed away in his room at Walter Reed Hospital, of congestive heart failure. Shortly afterwards his body was transferred to Washington DC, with the state funeral conducted on March 31st. (2)

There were over 2,000 guests at the funeral which included representatives from 78 countries from around the world. His body is now buried on the grounds of the Eisenhower Presidential Center in Abilene, Kansas ... but his soul and spirit is with his Lord and Savior Jesus Christ in Heaven.

Dwight Eisenhower (courtesy of: El Dorado Country Club)

Caption: Kiri Nguon (photo taken in San Diego, CA.)

Chapter 2

Cambodian Pro-Soccer Player's Escape From Pol Pot's Regime

K iri Nguon was born in Cambodia in August of 1952. Little did Kiri know that only around 20 years later his country would go down one of its darker paths which have been recorded in its history.

As a young boy Kiri grew up with his family in Cambodia's capital city of Phnom Penn. He lived in an environment that besides living with his mother and father, it would also include his uncles, aunts and his cousins. (1) The young boy would start playing soccer in his early teens.

It was also during Kiri's early childhood when King Sihanouk had come to power in Cambodia restoring the Khmer civilization to the royal line of leadership. During the majority of the 1800s Cambodia was ruled by Kings. By 1880 that all changed when Cambodia was incorporated into Indo-China, a French colony.

"Led by King Sihanouk, independence finally came in 1953". (2) For over a decade (from the late 1950s through the 1960s) the city of Phnom Penn and some rural communities as well were beginning to improve economically. It was also during this time when tourism throughout the country would improve also.

Despite the country's economic improvement there were elements of the government in the early '70s along with members of the Cambodian army who formed a resistance to the royal King's leadership. With the support of the North Vietnamese army and members of the Chinese Communist Party, the Khmer Rouge army became a power within the jungles and outlining villages of Cambodia.

By April of 1975 the Khmer Rouge began to take over the whole country. They garnered control over the population of seven million by intimidating and eliminating opponents of their regime. The Khmer Rouge government was completely totalitarian in nature and had zero tolerance for any resistance. During this period of time, many Cambodians were either persecuted, killed or would be eventually forced to flee their homeland.

Meanwhile, Kiri Nguon's family supported themselves by selling food in the central market of Phnom Penn. The family worshipped Buddha and practiced Confucius' teachings. As soccer was slowly gaining popularity in the country of Cambodia, Kiri began by regularly practicing the sport in middle school. He continued to play into high school and was ultimately assigned to a school that specialized in training gifted athletes. Ultimately, Kiri 's skills in soccer advanced him to a level where he was invited to play on the Cambodian International Youth Team. By 1973, his team participated in a tournament in Thailand. Kiri ultimately became a member of the Cambodian Army as a sports student. (1)

In 1974 Kiri was invited to join the Cambodian national team. It was during this era when the sport of soccer gained a huge following throughout the country. Kiri originally played on this team as a midfielder, changing later to playing defense for Cambodia's national team.

While playing on the national soccer team, Kiri lived in the sports complex in Phnom Penn, away from his family. Due to the rising danger of the new regime, Kiri decided to reunite with his family.

Asked by members of the Khmer Rouge when he expected to come back to Phnom Penn, Kiri informed them he was searching for relatives who he thought had gone into the surrounding countryside.

The regime forced thousands to leave the capital city of Phnom Penh to work the fields and farms in the country. During this purge, people were killed and tortured. Cambodians with any social prestige or stature prior to the Khmer Rouge's ascent into power were viewed suspiciously. Kiri was convinced that no one was safe under the Khmer Rouge.

Ultimately, Kiri located his mother and even some of his more distant relatives. They decided to leave Cambodia due to the social instability and threats to their lives caused by this new government and their leader Pol Pot.

The family fled to Vietnam, where Kiri worked as a fisherman. By late 1975, Kiri was living in Ho Chi Minh City. Soon afterwards Kiri reunited with some of his old team mates from Cambodia. He then became a member of the Vietnamese premier soccer league and was employed to play professionally (1) for several years. The league was supported and sponsored by a regional gasoline company.

Over time there were strong indications that communist Vietnam was intent on invading Cambodia. Considering his heritage and his prominence as a professional soccer player, Kiri thought it would be prudent to leave Vietnam. He considered taking a boat out of the country but government dictates allowed only boat owners to take their boats out to sea.

By 1979, Kiri decided Thailand was a safer destination than Cambodia. Kiri had become friends with a translator (1). He suggested to Kiri, if it was plausible, to travel by bus to Thailand. Kiri was well aware that this journey would be extremely dangerous. Whether by foot, bicycle, bus or automobile, he knew he had to travel through war-torn towns and provinces controlled by the Khmer Rouge or by the Communist army of Vietnam. Already he knew of a number of his former friends and acquaintances who had been murdered by the Khmer Rouge.

Kiri started his journey to Thailand with other refugees who had similar plans to leave Vietnam and Cambodia. The experience was not only terrifying for Kiri but opened up his eyes to the extreme cruelty of humans against their own country-men. Kiri once described this experience as similar to the imagery portrayed in the acclaimed movie-documentary, *The Killing Fields*.

Kiri crossed rice fields with his bicycle in his trip through Cambodia. A local farmer showed him how to avoid the soldier checkpoints on both the Vietnam and Cambodian sides of the border. He used his bicycle to travel on main roads as well, although some areas were destroyed by land mines. He stayed one night in a city in the province of Svay Rieng. The next morning he continued his journey to the capitol of Phnom Penh. He stayed there two days searching for a group to escape with to Thailand. Finally finding four men with two bicycles between them, they began their travel to Battambong province. From there they would head to the Thailand border.

Kiri needed to travel 200-300 km to get to the border. The Khmer Rouge was infamous for the deadly mines and sharpened, poisoned bamboo stakes buried on the trails throughout the remote countryside. Kiri had to be careful when travelling these remote but well-used trails. In just seconds, these buried mines could tear limbs from their victims, maiming or killing them. The Khmer Rouge sought to discourage refugees from escaping into Thailand in the most devastating ways possible.

In one episode outside of Batdambang providence, Khmer Rouge insurgents fired bazookas at a civilian bus that was, moments earlier, near Kiri. On his passage through New Camp 007, Kiri had to walk past scattered body parts on the roadside.

Kiri's group traded in their bicycles and went on foot. They needed to avoid soldiers from the Khmer Rouge. As they traveled through the jungle they found out that someone had been shot the day before in that area. Kiri met up with one of his old teammates from the town of

Sisophon who would lead them to the border. They walked across rice fields in the Makak valley and then again went deep into the jungle. It was vital to walk in single file on the trails due to the land mines. Kiri passed a human body near the trail confirming his worst fears.

Right after that, Kiri's party encountered Khmer Rouge soldiers with their AK 47's slung around their shoulders. One of them singled Kiri out and said to his buddy, "Look! That guy! Does he look like Chinese or Vietnamese?" When I heard him speak in Khmer I knew he was going to stop me, so I said to my friend, "Ah! Ya! Angkal bann daol?" Translated to, "Dude! Ya know when we get there?" Then I was able to pass.'

Hours later that evening they arrived at another camp with a new group of soldiers who were fighting against both the Khmer Rouge and the new government of Phnom Penn. It was only one week later when the Khmer Rouge occupied that camp, though Kiri never learned how many were killed.

Kiri and his fellow travelers providentially hitched a ride with an international Red Cross and UNHCR bus. The bus took them to the Koa I Dang refugee camp in Thailand, where he stayed for several months. Finally, Kiri had reached safety.

At the camp, Kiri was befriended by a group of Christian missionaries who spoke the Khmer language. Kiri was moved by the love of Christ shown by these missionaries, and decided to become a follower of his new Lord and Savior, Jesus Christ (3).

Thanks to the advice of his translator friend who had also escaped from Vietnam, Kiri moved to the Sikhiev camp (in Thailand) where he lived in a designated room with other Christian believers (1). It was there that Kiri discovered his calling to share the gospel.

With the assistance of the missionary group, Kiri traveled to Indonesia to learn English and possibly train for the ministry. This occurred between 1980 and 1981. He was interviewed a number of times until it was decided that the Christian and Missionary Alliance would sponsor him as a refugee. From there he was sent to the United States (1).

At that time (in the early 1980s) the United States customs office allowed supervised refugees to enter the United States if they were from a country where persecution was rampant. Obviously Cambodia and Vietnam qualified as such nations.

Kiri's sponsor flew him to Rhode Island via Thailand and Singapore. Kiri stayed in the home of a Cambodian family and worked as a repairman in Provident, R.I. He used some of the money he earned to pay back his sponsor for the cost of his travel to the United States. He also became involved with the Missionary Alliance Church in Rhode Island.

During the 1980s, the U.S. government required that a legal refugee had the right to become a citizen if he or she applied for citizenship and entered the country legally. He also knew that he had to reside legally in the United States for at least 5 years and follow the law before he would be considered a candidate for U.S. citizenship (1).

By 1986, Kiri moved from Provident, Rhode Island to California. Peter Song San, a friend of Kiri, spoke highly of the former Cambodian soccer player. Because of his extraordinary growth in his new found faith in Christ, it was decided to assign Kiri to the position of assistant pastor of the Christian and Missionary Alliance Church in Santa Rosa, California.

In 1986 Kiri moved to Santa Rosa, California to begin his new vocation. Over the course of the next year and a half he demonstrated an aptitude for ministering to people in the area. He was also mentored during this time by the senior pastor of the church.

The Alliance Church is located in Sonoma County which is north of the city of San Francisco. The church itself ministers to people from a variety of backgrounds around the county of Sonoma. They take pride in reaching out to people with God's love. In 1986 they were excited to add Kiri to their staff.

During the mid to late 1980s the United States was experiencing an increase of legal refugees from Cambodia. The federal government was aware of the hideous slaughter of Cambodians residents by both communist regimes in Cambodia and Vietnam. They responded by reaching out to many war-torn citizens from that South- East Asian country.

In 1987, it was estimated that there was a population of around eight thousand Cambodians living in San Diego County. It was during the prior year that Kiri met Joe Kong (who was a Superintendent of the Christian & Missionary Alliance Churches in the United States). It was his responsibility to oversee churches that specifically ministered to the estimated 300,000 Cambodians who lived across America.

Even though Kiri did not have experience as lead pastor, Mr. Kong suggested that now might be the time to start a new church in San Diego as a way to reach out to the Cambodian population there. Joe originally met Kiri when he was living in Santa Rosa so he decided to "invite him to move to San Diego to start a church." (5)

Joe Kong was also impressed with Kiri's passion to reach out to the Cambodian community where he was living. As a church Superintendent, he thought that Kiri's new assignment was perfect for his community.

The First Cambodian Evangelical Church was located near Laurel Street in San Diego. As a new senior pastor, Kiri was to lead that church from 1987 to 2000. It was a wonderful experience for the former professional soccer player.

In 2000, Kiri became senior pastor of the Cambodian Nazarene Church, also in San Diego. Church members were made up primarily of people from Cambodian descent. Some of these church members were former Khmer Rouge citizens who still had labor camp numbers tattooed on their arms.

Kiri had enjoyed his United States citizenship for over ten years and had built a strong foundation for the Cambodian community in San Diego. Still, Kiri reflected on Cambodia and the great spiritual need as well as the poverty of his former countrymen. Only around 4% of

Cambodians were Christian. By now, Kiri was talking to some of his peers about the possibility of becoming a missionary in their homeland.

With the growing popularity of various Christian organizations to reach out to young people through sports, Kiri thought it would be a good idea to use his soccer background to reach out to the Cambodian people for Christ.

He imagined that some of the old residents of Phnom Penn might remember him too. This fact could help him springboard into a soccer sports ministry. He also knew that God had more in store for him. In 2008, Kiri gathered up his possessions and embarked on his next great mission.

It was during this time period that the government of Cambodia was no longer controlled by a dictator. By the late-1990s Cambodia had become a Constitutional Monarchy. The government was essentially run by a "Council of Ministers, headed by the prime minister… Legislative power (was) vested in a bicameral legislature composed of the National Assembly which has the power to vote on draft law and the Senate which has the power to review… The judiciary was tasked with the protection of rights and liberties of the citizens." (4)

After studying the current state of affairs of his former country, Kiri knew that the social and political environment in Cambodia was now safe for him to start his ministry.

Over a number of months Kiri visited families in neighborhoods around Phnom Penn. He informed them that he was forming a soccer school and putting together a team where their sons could play soccer. He also located a soccer field in the suburbs where his teams could regularly practice.

Kiri's appeal to the community was warmly received by a variety of families around the city where he grew up. Young boys joined his team so as to learn and improve their soccer skills. It was this platform that allowed Kiri to gradually introduce the gospel to the boys, young men, and eventually to their families also!

Over a period of time, Kiri started Bible and prayer meetings with these families and their sons who were interested in their coach's message of love and grace as found in the Bible.

In Kiri's own words he describes his love for God. "There by the grace of God he found me and saved me through the blood of Jesus Christ in December 1979...I was born again Christian and now we know him by keeping all His words. Thank Jesus for his loving kindness. Amen."

The sports missionary ministry that Kiri Nguon established in Cambodia in 2008 has now been ongoing for over 14 years. He has since made several visits back to California during that time period. In one such visit to the United States, Kiri set up a non-profit forum where fellow believers can donate to his well-deserved ministry via *International Church Missions*. Donations go towards Kiri's ministry that is reaching out to people with the gospel in a country where sadly there still is a very small Christian population. It is also a county that is considered to be one of the poorest countries in the world. The average salary for those working in Phnom Penn is only $290 a month.

The way you can help support Kiri's outreach efforts is by donating to: International Church Missions, P.O. Box 4550, Oceanside, CA 92052 noting Kiri Nguon & Cambodian Sports Ministry as the recipient of your gift. It will certainly be appreciated! God bless!

website: www.harvestallianceintl.org

Chapter 3

Rock Hudson & His Amazing Commitment To Christ Just Days Before His Death

R ock Hudson, (whose birth name was Roy Harold Scherer), was born in Winnetka, Illinois on November 17th, 1925. His father, Roy Scherer, lost his job as an auto mechanic during the early years of the Great Depression. Sadly, Roy's father left his family when Roy was a small child. In 1933 Roy's mother remarried and Roy's last name became Fitzgerald. Unfortunately, the young boy did not get along with his new step-father. (1)

During his teenage years Roy attended New Trier High School in Winnetka. He graduated from that school in the spring of 1943. During his high school years Roy worked as an usher in the town's local theater. Roy realized he was drawn to movies and the entertainment industry. He dreamed of a career in acting, but World War II took precedence.

After graduation, Roy enlisted in the US Navy. He was assigned to train at the Great Lakes Naval Training facility. He was then sent to San Francisco to board the naval ship, SS Lew Wallace, in route to the Philippines. Roy trained and ultimately served as an aircraft mechanic until after the conclusion of the war. In 1946 Roy obtained an honorable discharge from the U.S. Navy.

Upon his discharge, the young man decided to move to Los Angeles in order to live with his biological father. During this time he sampled a number of different types of jobs settling in as a truck driver around the county of Los Angeles.

In his free time, Roy passed out pictures of himself including his contact information outside the gates of movie studios around town. Roy thought that his efforts might be rewarded as there were a number of movie producers who worked in these local studios. (1)

In 1947, Roy was contacted by Henry Wilson, a local talent agent. Upon the advice of his talent agent, Roy changed his name to Rock Hudson. (2)

Part of Rock's initial problem in breaking into the acting field was that the twenty-three year old had no prior acting experience or training. Nevertheless in 1948, Rock's talent agent was able to get him a contractual acting job with Warner Brothers. His first film with them was *Fire Squadron,* where his small role was not credited.

In 1949 Hudson's employment contract with Warner Brothers was sold by the film company to Universal Pictures. It was there where Hudson was given a number of opportunities to garner the skills he needed in order to be a successful Hollywood actor. Rock's first accredited film part was in the movie *Undertow.* He continued to play bit parts in a number of films for the next few years which honed his acting skills. These films included the 1950 release of the films: *Peggy, Winchester '73* and *Desert Hawk.* The 1951 releases included the films: *Tomahawk, Fat Man* and *Bright Victory.* (2)

It was during this relatively short time period that Rock Hudson graduated from playing bit roles in various films to procuring the lead role in the movie *Magnificent Obsession.*

In 1955 Hudson married the young, aspiring young actress Phyllis Gates. Then, in 1956 Hudson received an Academy Award nomination for his part in the film, *Giant*. That film also featured actors James Dean and Elizabeth Taylor. (1)

In 1957, Hudson starred in the film, *A Farewell to Arms*. During this same year the young actor's two year marriage to Phyllis Gates ended.

It was also during that same year when Rock met singer/actor Pat Boone in a fitting room at one of their film studios. According to Pat, "they didn't ever really hang out together they, over time, became acquaintances." Pat later said in a phone interview that he and Rock would see each other from time to time at various Hollywood events around Los Angeles. (3)

It had now become clear that the young thirty-five year old actor was becoming quite a box office draw in Hollywood. In the decade of the 1960s, Hudson stared in a number of popular movies. They included *Pillow Talk*, *Lover Come Back*, *Send Me No Flowers* and *Ice Station Zebra*. Other films during this decade included *Blindfold*, *Seconds*, *Tubruk*, *Fine Pair* and *The Undefeated* with actor John Wayne.

Hudson continued to appear in a number of Hollywood films during the 1960s. It also became clear to those around him that the actor was gay. He had a variety of relationships, which was common knowledge in the Hollywood community. However his agent, Henry Wilson, would use numerous strategies to keep his client's reputation unstained and out of the headlines.

Altogether Rock Hudson was in a total of sixty-five films. This doesn't include his appearances as an actor in several television series or his 70+ appearances on live T.V. shows.

During the 1970s, Hudson starred (along with actress Susan Saint James) in the popular TV series *McMillan and Wife*. This successful NBC series ran from 1971 to 1977. The television series revolved around the exploits of police commissioner Steward McMillan and his detective wife. (2)

It was also during the late 1970s and '80s when the movie actor became heavily involved in drinking and smoking. In November of 1981, the obvious decline in his health resulted in a heart attack, requiring quintuple heart bypass surgery. Despite his health issues, the fifty-six year old continued to smoke.

During the next decade, the actor kept working. He appeared in several TV movies including *World War III* as well as the film *The Ambassador* which was filmed in Israel.

In 1984, the fifty-nine year old actor accepted a part in the on-going television series *Dynasty*. His character, Daniel Reese, acted as the love interest for Krystle Carrington (who was played by actress Linda Evans). However, it became obvious to those around him that his health was worsening. He had difficulty speaking his lines, and had resumed using cue cards.

The producers of this television show eventually made the decision to write him off the cast of the *Dynasty* TV series. (2a) It wasn't too long after this fateful event when Rock would formerly announce he had AIDS. His announcement was publicized on July 25th, 1985. With his announcement Rock Hudson became one of the first celebrities to ever make such a formal proclamation in Hollywood. (1)

It was also during the fall of 1985 when Pat Boone's wife, Shirley, was conducting weekly bible studies in her home. According to her husband Pat, their home was only about a five minute drive from Rock's house in Beverly Hills. Two of the attendees at the meetings were nurses who were currently caring for Rock, and both were believers in Christ. (3)

According to Mr. Boone, in an interview that was conducted on July 16, 2021 – he stated that both nurses shared Christ with the actor. One of the nurses informed Shirley that she had led him to Christ.

It wasn't too long after this when Pat and Shirley arranged through one of the nurses to get permission to visit the movie star in his home. They both arrived around 8pm. Pat noticed that Rock was so emaciated he could hardly recognize him.

During this particular evening Pat prayed fervently for his friend. As Pat reported in his interview, Rock was receptive to them. Pat also told his friend that night that: "the Bible talks about (anointing) oil… I will make a sign of the cross on your chest with oil, if that is OK with you?" Silently the fifty-nine year old actor removed his pajama top and "allowed (Pat) to do this."

Clearly this was an act of faith on Pat and Shirley's part. They were hopeful that the Lord would heal Rock. That same evening, Tom, Rock's friend and caretaker felt their prayer had a positive and uplifting affect.

In the morning of October 2, 1985, Pat contacted the Rev. Terrance Sweeney, PhD to see if he could immediately come over to Rock Hudson's home in Beverly Hills. It was a little after noon when he arrived as confirmed by a phone interview with Rev. Sweeney (4). While Rock was still alive he could only nod or blink his eyes to communicate.

Rev. Sweeney performed the Catholic Last Rights Ceremony with the fifty-nine year old actor. This seemed fitting, since when Rock was young and living in Winnetka, he and his family attended the local Catholic Church.

Rev. Sweeney also confirmed by phone that he felt that Rock Hudson had acknowledged his sins and accepted God's grace. The fifty-nine year old actor died later that day.

It was to become a shock to Pat and his wife to discover that their friend had died so suddenly. Although saddened, they felt strongly that Rock was with the Lord. While Rock could only nod and blink his eyes as a sign of acceptance, they both knew that God had touched his life.

When you read the account of Jesus' death on the cross, remember the man who was crucified next to Christ. On the same day when he was crucified along with Christ, the other man knew he was doomed. Nevertheless, he asked Jesus (who was crucified next to him) "Remember me when you come into your kingdom". Jesus answered, "Truly, I tell you today you will be with me in paradise." (Luke 23:42-43)

This singular expression of God's love was also demonstrated in the last days of this famous actor's life. Though Rock Hudson strayed far from God, God lovingly drew him back to Himself a few days before his death.

This clearly goes to show us all: If you have a friend who is far from God's love, keep praying for him or her. Don't give up! Our dear Lord can reach anyone who is open to receive His love and His grace.

> "For God so loved the world that He gave His only begotten Son that whosoever believes in Him shall not perish but have everlasting life." (John 3:16)

Rock Hudson (courtesy of TCM movies)

27

Rock Hudson star on Hollywood Blvd, Los Angeles

Caption: Lawrence Hill

Chapter 4

Lawrence Hill – Oh Happy Day

L awrence Hill, as a choir member destined to record the top single *Oh Happy Day*, took an interesting path to discover that happy day in his own life.

Born the son of Pastor William E. and Evangelist Deolla Hill of the Powerhouse Church of God in Christ in San Pablo, California, Lawrence was raised in a godly family in Oakland, California. Lawrence was a member of the church choir and played the cello during his junior and senior high school years. In 1963, when he was only 14, he had an opportunity to sing with a Christian group called 'The Heavenly Tones' with the now American award winning gospel singer Tramaine Hawkins.

Lawrence and a group of his friends would join the Northern California State Youth Choir (NCSYC). Edwin Hawkins and Betty Watson were the choir directors. Hawkins, a member of the Ephesians Church of God in Christ, and Betty Watson invited singers from other local Church of God in Christ churches to join the NCSYC singing group. The choir was organized to inspire youth everywhere. The NCSYC had also participated in many musical events, as well as concert engagements at colleges, auditoriums and churches. The choir included almost fifty members (2). During 1967 the choir recorded many of the songs that would appear in their first album; including *Oh Happy Day* and *Let us go into the House of the Lord*. The choir recorded their first album on the Century 70 custom label. The NCSYC would later change its name.

Lawrence attended Berkeley High School, during an era when the Black Panther movement was gaining popularity. He and some of his friends participated in the movement's protests including a sit-in at Berkeley High School. Lawrence and his friends were concerned about the plight of Black Americans and the plight that too many Black families were dependent on welfare. After graduating from Berkeley High, Lawrence began his freshman year (in the fall of '68) at Linfield College in McMinnville, Oregon.

It was only a month after starting college that Lawrence's mother Deolla unexpectedly passed away. Lawrence flew to Oakland for the funeral and wake. Despite his father's request that he stay home, Lawrence decided to return to Linfield to continue his college education.

At Linfield, Lawrence became involved in the college's Action Committee, a support group for African American students. Eventually Lawrence became president of the committee. He was also involved in social events at the school, including the normal college beer parties.

As Lawrence was busily immersed in college life, one day he turned on the radio and was stunned to hear the Edwin Hawkins singers *Oh Happy Day* recording on the air. (The Northern California State Youth Choir had been renamed The Edwin Hawkins Singers.) The recording was initially discovered by a DJ working for a KSAN Underground rock station. The DJ happened to select that song, and almost overnight it became a hit. (1) The news of the popularity of recording spread resulting in the choir members reuniting, including Lawrence. The choir would then sign with the Pavilion label in 1969 for their second album: *He's a Friend of Mine*.

Meanwhile, *Oh Happy Day* sold over one million copies in just two months. The song made it to the pop charts; making an international mark in singles charts as well. It reached #4 on the United States charts and, #1 in France, Germany and the Netherlands. It made #2 in the singles charts in the United Kingdom, Canada and Ireland. Upon Lawrence's return to Oakland, he was ecstatic to receive his first royalty check. (1) In June of 1969, the Edwin Hawkins Singers began a year tour around the country, performing before thousands.

Eventually, Lawrence returned to Oakland to attend Merritt Junior College with the intention of transferring to the University of California at Berkeley. He formed a new music group, the New Generation Singers, and eventually moved to Los Angeles. In LA, he became a staff writer for Capital & Shelter Records. Lawrence's job enabled him to work with a variety of musicians and song writers including Motown artist and writer Gloria Jones, rock star David Bowie, and T-Rex. Lawrence also performed as a background singer and musician for Leon Russell by touring with him for nine months.

In a career switch, Lawrence snagged a job with the County of Los Angeles. He was promoted in the District Attorney's offices department to the position as a Child Support Officer. His duties were to enforce court orders for thousands of clients (1). During this time he was also a lobbyist for SEIU (Service Employee International Union), as well as a member of the county's Oversight and Advisory Committee for Child Support.

It was also during this time when Lawrence began to fall away from his father's church and religion. William Hill had left his church in northern California to accept a position as associate pastor for a large church in Los Angeles, but Lawrence could not be persuaded to attend. As Lawrence admits, it was during this time in his life that he was "living on the wild side." (1)

One evening in 1984, as Lawrence was taking a shower, he had an encounter that was to rock his world. While showering, he began singing the song: *Blessed Assurance*. Suddenly, he felt the overwhelming presence of Almighty God, and collapsed in the intensity of this experience. With the presence of God permeating his room, Lawrence surrendered his life right then and there to his Lord and Savior. Later, Lawrence recounted: "the anointing was on me so heavily that it was a transformative period of my life". (1) Looking back, Lawrence realized that the Lord had been faithfully pursuing him all those years.

After this life-altering encounter, Lawrence discovered that his father and friends had been praying for him for years. His rendezvous with God during that remarkable night helped to firmly establish his personal relationship with his Lord and Savior Jesus Christ.

Lawrence continued his work as a Child Support Officer for the County of Los Angeles. He also had the opportunity to team up with writer and producer Thomas Campbell, music director of the TV series *Touched by an Angel*. Lawrence became choir master for a portion of the series and arranged a majority of songs for star Della Reese. (1) He also worked as a vocal sound designer for Eves Bayou, Caveman Valentine, and singer and voiceover actor Sister/Sister.

Lawrence also completed his certified courses in Independent Record Label Administration at UCLA. In his free time he was involved in the music ministries of six different churches around Los Angeles. He assisted the Brown Memorial A.M.E. Church in developing and directing their choir. Lawrence also led the music department at the Walke Temple A.M.E. church from 2001 to 2004, and later developed the music department at the First Lutheran Church in Inglewood, California. In 2007 Lawrence worked for the Messiah Church in Los Angeles in a Minister of Music position. As he continued to help various churches, Lawrence worked as a background singer, arranger and writer for the New Generation Singers, James Cleveland, Patti Labelle and Della Reese. By 2014 Lawrence became the music minister for the Sunnyside Baptist Church.

Eventually Lawrence started his own record label: Inheritance Records. He viewed this new independent label as a way "to share with the world gospel artists that traditional major labels would not give the attention needed for new and upcoming recording artists."(1) Lawrence decided he wanted to focus all his attention on the new label, as he retired from the County of Los Angeles. He sold his home in

California and moved to the state of Georgia. Lawrence has now put together a website involving this new assignment from God. www. InheritanceRecords.com

This website is designed to make gospel music readily available to people across the country. It also serves as a platform where solo artists as well as other Christian music groups can record and make their music available to the public.

Despite all the years Lawrence spent in church singing songs to God, he had never encountered Him personally until that one unexpected moment in time some years ago. His knowledge of God up to that point was all about his father's relationship with him. One evening God encountered Lawrence and the connection became his own. Finally, *Oh Happy Day* became an actuality in Lawrence Hill's own life.

Chapter 5

Gary Puckett's Life Journey

Gary Puckett was born on October 17th, 1942 in Hibbing, Minnesota. Gary was the first of five siblings born to Arlon and Leona Puckett. His parents met in high school near Pelican Rapids, Minnesota. During World War II Gary's father served in the European Theater of the war but was ultimately imprisoned in a German war camp. He was freed by Allied Forces after six months.

It was also during the war when Gary and his mother lived with his grandfather in Pelican Rapids, Minnesota. When Gary's father finally returned home after the war, he decided to pursue a career in merchandizing. This led him to a job with Allied Corporation in Watertown, South Dakota. That job was followed by another in the same field in the state of Washington. From 1946 to 1959, the Puckett's were to add four more children to the family; two boys and two girls.

Gary's parents shared a passion for music. His mother, Leona, regularly played the piano. His father expressed his own passion for music as a local barbershop quartet singer. Leona tried to teach her son how to play the piano while Gary was still in grade school, but Gary later admitted that he found the guitar "more to his sensibilities".(1)

After the family's move to the state of Washington, Gary attended high school in the town of Yakima. By his senior year in high school, the family had relocated to Twin Falls, Idaho. Gary graduated from Twin Falls High School in Idaho.

In 1960, Gary's father seized on an opportunity to work for the Meulling Department Store in the Pacific Beach, a suburb of San Diego, California. And so, the family moved again, this time to California. There, Gary attended San Diego City College. While Gary enjoyed some of the classes he was enrolled in, he became frustrated with school because what he really wanted to do was to become a musician.(1)

Instead of continuing his schooling at San Diego City College, the young man vowed to pursue a career in music. Gary joined a local band. Over the next few years he played in a number of venues around the county, playing with several bands ranging in size from four to twelve members.

Within a couple of years the young musician joined a band called the *Outcasts*. The group was comprised of bassist Kerry Chater, keyboardist Gary 'Mutha' Withem, tenor saxophonist Dwight Bement and drummer Paul Wheatbread (2). In 1966, drummer Paul Wheatbread moved to Los Angeles to work as drummer for the television show: *Where the Action Is*. The TV show featured a variety of rock groups from around the country.

Gary and his band, the *Outcasts* continued performing in San Diego at The Quad. The group toured in the Pacific Northwest as well.(3) It wasn't too long before the group compiled a portfolio of music, lyrics and demo tapes which they recorded in Los Angeles. It was also during this time when Jerry Fuller, a producer from CBS records, decided to attend several of Gary's concerts at The Quad in San Diego.

Fuller was impressed with Gary's vocals as well as the band's ability to play and work together musically. In a meeting with the band and their manager, Fuller confirmed that Columbia wanted to sign the musicians to a recording contract. Their agreement, however, was contingent on the group's willingness to focus their talent towards their recording contract and ballad formula. (2)

Under manager Dick Badger, the music band was renamed *Gary Puckett and The Union Gap* in early 1967 (3). Gary and the *Outcasts* musicians formed the nucleus of this new band. Their producer believed the band could attract a large following of listeners who enjoyed their unique rock sound.

In order to set them apart from other rock groups, Gary and the rest of the band's members decided to dress in Civil War uniforms during their performances.

In August of 1967, The Union Gap recorded and released their first single, *Woman, Woman*. Radio Host Bob Harrington from WCOL, a popular Ohio radio station, liked the single and featured it regularly on his program. As it turned out, this opening single became a national success for Gary Puckett and the Union Gap. It reached the top ten and sold over 1 million copies.

With Jerry Fuller as their producer and writer, the group signed with Columbia Records in June of 1967. Gary and his band also released a series of four albums which additionally bolstered their popularity. From 1968 to early 1970 Gary and his band would begin to tour and perform across the country

In February of '68, their single *Young Girl* reached #1 nationally according to *Cashbox Magazine* and # 2 nationally according to *Billboard*. It was their second million selling record. Gary and his band released three more hit singles that year. *Lady Willpower* was released in May which also went to number 1 according to *Cashbox;* and *Over You*, which was released in August, reached #7 nationally on the Billboard charts.

Gary Puckett and the Union Gap took advantage of their popularity by continuing to tour. They played in a variety of venues from states all across the country. In 1969, the Union Gap released two more singles: *Don't Give into Him*, which reached #15 on the charts and also *This Girl is a Woman Now* which reached the top ten on Billboard's national chart. It was also in July of 1970 that Columbia Records released the album: *Gary Puckett and the Union Gap's Greatest Hits*.

In 1970 the band's management decided to change the way they would pay members of the music group. Instead of getting a percentage of the group's total revenue, band members were to receive a weekly salary. This new arrangement resulted in several members of the group opting to leave the band. It was around this same time that Gary, as lead vocalist, ventured into working as a solo act with musical support provided by several members of his former band. The last performance by Gary and his two remaining band members took place at the Orange County fairgrounds in 1971. (3)

The 29 year old musician began to strongly consider pursuing a career in acting. He performed in theatrical productions around Los Angeles and began studying acting as a career. In one of his acting classes, Gary acted out a scene from a movie. It was during this time when he discovered a book about Transcendental Meditation and its founder, Maharishi Mahesh Yogi. After reading the book, Gary was inspired to start meditating regularly. (1)

After having little success in his pursuit of becoming an actor, Gary decided to once again move back to San Diego from Los Angeles. Once back in San Diego Gary performed as a solo act in various venues around the city. He also continued to meditate and practice Transcendental Meditation.

By 1983, Gary decided to return to Los Angeles. He had discovered, (along with a number of other popular rock groups from the 60's), that there was still interest in his music as oldies radio stations had begun to pursue him. Gary was approached by an entertainment/music advisor who worked with other well-known '60s music groups to put together a series of concerts. In April '84 Puckett formed a new band and began an eight month tour.

One day in 1985 while Gary was meditating he heard God's voice. He distinctly recalled the moment: "God spoke to me and said 'get up and walk away from Maharishi and I will show you the Way'." (1) This revelation touched Gary's heart even though initially he was conflicted by his desire to make a comeback.

Within the next one and a half years Gary and his band would again tour. This concert tour included the rock bands: the *Monkees, Herman's Hermits* and the *Grass Roots*. The concert tour which celebrated the 20 year reunion for many of these musicians, turned out to be very well received. The tour lasted six and a half months.

In 1988 Gary was again performing, this time in Florida. It was there, at one of the local venues that he first met Lorrie (Haimes), who was to later become the love of his life. Born in Philadelphia in 1959, Lorrie moved to Florida in 1977 where she ran her own business.

Gary again relocated back to San Diego. Once in San Diego, he vividly recalled his experience of hearing God five years earlier. He admitted that it took him five years to make a commitment to Christ. (1) He began attending Horizon Christian Fellowship which was led, at that time, by senior pastor Mike Macintosh. He also went to Maranatha Church in Rancho Bernardo which was located closer to his home. His attendance at both of these Bible based churches encouraged Gary to grow in his new found faith in Christ.

Gary realized that he had been richly blessed in life. He was also grateful that his old friend, Grant Goodeve (the actor from the *Eight is Enough* TV show) had faithfully encouraged him to pursue his belief in Christ. As a new believer, Gary found spiritual strength by regularly reading his Bible morning and night and praying regularly to his Creator.(1)

During the '90s, Gary and Lorrie visited one another intermittently. In 1998 they were reunited at one of Gary's concerts. Even though Gary was a California resident living in Rancho Bernardo, he decided to propose to Lorrie and move to Florida. In the year 2000 Gary sold his home, made the trek to Florida and during that same year the couple were married. As for his belief in God and the Bible, it was now stronger than ever! It turned out that Lorrie is a strong believer in Christ also.

In 2001 Gary released a solo album entitled *Gary Puckett at Christmas*. During the next eighteen years Gary occasionally performed in a variety of live concerts featuring other oldies music bands. In his free time he enjoys his life, family and ongoing relationship with his Lord and Savior. Gary and Lorrie now have two daughters, and three grandchildren.

Today, Gary and his band's music (from the late '60s and early '70s) are still popular. From 2012 to 2013 Gary and his band participated in the 'Happy Together' music tour with other bands by noting that each year the band's level of participation changes. (1) In 2022 Gary and his band again performed around the country with the 'Happy Again Tour' which would also feature other '60s music bands such as the *Turtles*, the *Association* and the *Cowsills*.

Gary proudly recognizes the importance of his faith in Christ. He and his wife Lorrie gladly acknowledge that their dear Lord and Savior Jesus Christ have made their lives much more meaningful to each of them. For this, they give God the glory!

Gary Puckett & the Union Gap (the Ed Sullivan Show)

Caption: Prince Chapel by the Sea AME church, La Jolla, CA.

Chapter 6

La Jolla's Early History And A Church That Touched The Lives Of Residents From The African American Community

B ack in 1850, the lands around the community of La Jolla, CA were officially incorporated by the county of San Diego. Recognizing the future potential of this coastal community were developers like Frank Botsford and investors like Gerald Heald who bought land around the community over a period of time during the late 1800s. Their investments and the realization of the attraction of this coastal town encouraged others to do so themselves.

By the early 1900's newspaper heiress Ellen Browning Scripps settled in the coastal community as well. She was enormously generous with her wealth as the local community would later recognize. Her gifts helped to create the Scripps Institute of Oceanography, the original Scripps Hospital, the La Jolla Recreational Center, the Women's Club, the Children's Pool (a designated park in the cove area) as well as the land which is now where the Torrey Pines State Park is located. By then, the community's population increased from around 350 residents in 1900 to over 4,000 by the end of World War I.

It was also during these first two decades that the African- American population in La Jolla would form and grow as well. It became obvious to outsiders that the early growth and development of La Jolla attracted a population who sought work in a variety of fields. "Blacks were drawn to the area because of the abundance of domestic service jobs." (1) They worked, lived, and would own property and even managed some businesses in La Jolla as well.

One of the first African-American residents in La Jolla was Thomas Debose. He came to the area in 1892. By 1897 he would buy along with his son-in-law (William Shannon) four unimproved lots in La Jolla for $100. According to research conducted by Lorenza Pace, "Henrietta Vanhorn was the first black female to settle in La Jolla." (2) Due to her work as a housekeeper, cook and independent laundry cleaner, she was able to purchase land in the La Jolla Park subdivision in 1887.

Realizing that she needed help to grow her business, Henrietta asked some of her relatives to assist her in her laundry business by joining her in La Jolla. By 1917 three of her relatives from back east would join Henrietta and move into her residence on Prospect Street in La Jolla.

Over time a number of black families would call La Jolla their home. They found that the area was ripe with opportunities for employment and self-employed business opportunities as well. Edgar Coleman was one of them. He came from the state of Arkansas. Over time he bought several lots which (due to zoning regulations) allowed him to move several cottages and housing units on to his property. Ultimately, these facilities allowed a number of his black friends to move to La Jolla where they would also find work.

Lorenza Pace's family's ties to La Jolla dates back to her grandfather becoming a local resident in the coastal community. Her grandfather, Ed Coleman, moved to La Jolla around 1917. He worked in a variety of jobs over the years ranging from a gardener, to a janitor and finally as a local realtor.

Over time Coleman would inform his relatives of the fine opportunities there were in this small coastal town. Agreeing with her father,

Madie Lee Coleman (Lorenza's mother) decided it would be good for her family to leave Chicago and move to this small San Diego coastal community too. By 1934 Madie gave birth to her daughter Lorenza at her family's house on Draper Street where Lorenza lived for over 20 years.

Ed Coleman was a dedicated follower of Christ. He not only had a positive spiritual influence on his daughter, Madie, but on his grand-daughter as well. As Lorenza would later say, "Nothing else was more important to her (her mother: Madie) than church and her faith." Madie's faith in Christ and the Bible would also positively influence Lorenza's other siblings too.

Lorenza fondly remembers the time when her mother encouraged her children to read their Bibles regularly at home. Looking back, Lorenza was intrigued about the positive spiritual influence her mother would have on a number of other local African-American residents too.

The church they attended would ultimately provide a rich history for their local community. It was during the early 1920s when the La Jolla African-American community had grown to over 22 residents. With their population continuing to grow, many African-American residents recognized the need to open a local church near their homes. By 1921, a church was formed.

Initially the church was called the La Jolla Union Mission. "Rev. Virgil McPherson came to La Jolla in 1926 to pastor the ... first black church in La Jolla. - Pastor McPherson and his wife lived in the small cottage at the rear end of the church property at 7519 Cuvier Street. A new building was eventually erected at the front of the property that became the sanctuary." (2)

"McPherson set up youth programs at the church to get young people interested in coming." (2). He put together a variety of events including beach parties, bicycle rides and programs to help kids with their home-work in his effort to attract young people to his church. Pastor McPherson served his church until May 6, 1938 when he passes away.

By 1943, the church's affiliation had changed to the African Methodist Episcopal (AME) denomination. This explains the name change to the

Prince Chapel by the Sea AME. The Church building located on Cuvier Street in La Jolla is on the same site and location as the original church that first began in the 1920s. Located next to the Bishops school which began operation in 1909, the church's location is a well-known site in the community.

Currently the church is led by the Reverend Denise Jackson who has been the leader of the Prince Chapel by the Sea since October of 2018. According to an article in the local newspaper, the *La Jolla Light*, "Jackson is only the second female pastor in Prince Chapel's history. The first was her mom, Reverend Annie Watson."

Denise was born in Rapid City, South Dakota. During the early stages of her life she lived in a variety of locations because her father served in the U.S. military. By 1973 her family moved to San Diego.

Denise remembers that by the age of 12, she had accepted Christ as her Savior. During that young age she was heavily influenced in her faith by her mother. Over time Annie would also have a positive influence in her community as well.

Denise would later recount an experience she had while she was attending Patrick Henry High School in San Diego. "I was on 4th and Broadway. I was standing on the corner getting ready to cross the street and catch the bus. The way I can describe it is like the sun ray hit me. And when I looked up in the sky, I could hear God calling me. And I remember my response was: not me at 16?" (3)

Clearly the Lord God reached out to Denise that day. It later became clear to Denise that the Lord was calling her into the ministry. However during the next few years the young woman was overwhelmed by some of the struggles her mother had experienced while she was involved in the ministry.

By this time, Denise was working part-time while attending college (at National University in San Diego). She graduated from the college with a degree in Behavioral Science. Ultimately she was hired by the federal government, working for the United States Department of Justice in San Diego, CA.

By the mid-1990s Denise distinctly remembers being called again by her loving God to serve in the ministry. This time she said "yes to Him" while she was residing in her apartment in Pasadena, California. When she said "yes" to the Lord that day, she remembers by recalling "that there was a release that came over me" that evening. She "finally realized that (she) had to accept His calling." With this realization she began to cry by telling her Lord "yes, yes!" while knowing that "a big burden was lifted off" her shoulders. (4)

In 1996, while still living in Pasadena, Denise would formally enter the 'Class on Instruction' in the AME church. From 1996 to 1997, she attended the First AME church in Pasadena, CA. Over time Denise would learn how to become a pastor for the church organization she decided to associate with. The AME church's 'Class on Instruction' is designed to prepare future church leaders for the ministry. It was also around this time when Denise was ordained as Deacon in the AME church.

While enrolled in the program, Denise still worked full time for the government. Clearly over time, she'd spiritually benefited each week from the AME program. Ultimately it would help her reach her goal of becoming a minister.

By 2012, Denise transferred back to San Diego with her federal government employer after requesting a job transfer. It was also in San Diego where Denise would officially complete her AME ministerial program.

Initially Denise became associated with the Bethel AME church on 30th & K Street in San Diego. She would serve that church as one of their Associate Ministers. Within a relatively short period of time, she would be assigned as Pastor for the Johnson Chapel AME church in El Centro, CA. With her new church assignment, Denise transferred to another government job this time being in Imperial County. (4)

Over time Denise had successfully learned how to be a well-trained Pastor. By the fall of 2017, Denise would again move back to San Diego County. As a 'Cum Laude' graduate from National University, Denise was now also an experienced pastor with AME church.

By October of 2018 Reverend Jackson became the Senior Pastor of Prince Chapel by the Sea A.M.E. church in La Jolla. As a strong believer in Christ, Rev. Jackson is fully committed to bless the church which she currently serves. She wants people in her church and the community to know about their Lord and Savior Jesus Christ. She also wants people to know Christ is (their) source of power, strength, joy and hope in life. (4)

Currently Denise is pursuing a 'Master of Theological Studies' degree. She is also the author of the book: '60 Ways to Save Your Home from Foreclosure' that was published in 2014.

Rev. Jackson understands the importance of inspiring her congregation. Her church has a wonderful music ministry which is also supported by wonderful vocalists and supporting musicians. Her congregation will always welcome guests to their Sunday 9am services at 7517 Cuvier Street in La Jolla, CA. You can find more about this fine church by going to their website at www.princechapelame.org.

Additionally Denise understands and appreciates the wonderful history of her church along with the African American history in their community. Additionally the City of San Diego has recognized the importance of the history of this church which was established in the 1920s by designating the church's street location as a historical site.

Lorenza Pace and some of her friends have worked to preserve, keep and retain a well-researched record of the black families and their descendants who moved into this coastal community for over the last century. Much of the detailed information of this history can be found in the fourth edition of Lorenza Pace's book: 'La Jolla California Black Pioneers & Pioneer Descendants 1880-1974'.

* I want to personally thank Ms. Pace for providing me access to this fine book.

Chapter 7

Mickey Rooney's Life-Changing Encounter With A Messenger From God

M ickey Rooney was born in Brooklyn New York, on September 23rd, 1920. His given name was Joseph Yule Jr. His father, Joe Yule, originally came from Scotland, while his mother, Nell Carter was born in Arkansas.

Nell had a tough life, as she, along with her sister and two brothers were orphaned as children. This eventually resulted in her joining a traveling show so she could help support herself and her family. Nell and Joe were both part of Vaudeville acts, which is how they met. Joe, as well, came from a humble background, and the couple soon married.

After Mickey was born, Nell went back to work four short weeks later. Since his parents were both in the entertainment business, Mickey later recalled spending "a good deal of time backstage, sleeping in a tray in the baggage trunk and waking when the spotlights (of the stage) flashed around". (1)

At a very early age, Mickey was drawn to the stage. This young boy and future film star knew that "the theater was an unusual nursery. Instead of blocks (he) played with props." (2) He began performing with his parents in the Vaudeville acts when he was less than two years old. His first appearance involved crawling across the floor in a tux.

When Mickey was only four years old his parents decided to separate. As the future film actor later recounted in his book, *Life is Too Short*: "I finally realized what the trouble was when, after a show one night, mom caught dad backstage in a compromising position with one of the other girls." (3)

Nell and Mickey moved to Kansas to live with Nell's sister Edna. Nell supported her little family by starting a business offering fried chickens for sale. She eventually sold the business and with the proceeds purchased a Model T Ford. Due to Nell and Mickey's past acting experience she decided to take a chance in Hollywood. Nell packed up the Model T and the little family was off to make a new start. Nell decided to visit a variety of studios around Hollywood for employment opportunities. As it turned out she ended up getting two jobs (outside of the entertainment business) so that she and her son could survive in Los Angeles. Eventually Nell saved up enough money to enroll her son in Mack's Dance Studio. It was not only a smart move but it introduced Mickey to Will Morrissey who "made a living in Hollywood by showcasing young talent." (4)

By this time Nell's son was five years old, he entered 1st grade at the Logan Street School. Nell saw an advertisement for a child actor, and took her son to a film producer by the name of Larry Darmour. He wanted to start a film series that would compete with the popular comedy series, *Our Gang*. Film executives understood the popularity of this series of short films which featured young neighborhood children like the *Our Gang* series characters Spanky, Alfalfa and Buckwheat.

The producer of a new competing film episode, *The McGuire* series needed a young, little guy to play the lead role of Mickey McGuire. After a number of cast meetings, Darmour gave the role of 'Mickey' to Nell's son. Both Nell and her son were thrilled with the news.

As it turned out the *Mickey McGuire* series involved shooting over seventy short films which would run from 1927 to 1936. It would mark the beginning of the actor's long film career. The series became so popular that Mickey along with his mother decided to change his first name from Joseph to Mickey. It was the studio's publicity man, Kenneth Wilson, who suggested that Mickey should also change his last name. He reasoned that the name Mickey Yule was less appealing, as "the rhythm was wrong." (5) Wilson suggested a name ending with a 'y' in it, hence the last name: Rooney.

Despite Mickey's new success in the film industry, this period of his life was trying for him because of his overall lack of focus in school. Eventually his mother thought it was best for Mickey to attend Ma Lawlor's` Professional School and Academy'.

During this same period of time, Nell remarried, this time to a man named Wynn Brown. Mickey was excited by the marriage, now he would have a father again.

In 1933 Mickey had performed in 6 films, and by 1934 in nine more (6). Even as a young actor, Mickey thought that during this time he was beginning to have a more normal life. He spent time with his new father fishing and attending local baseball and football games. He cherished his time spent with Wynn.

However there was a day when Wynn came to the young boy and much to his dismay, he told Mickey that he and his mother, Nell, were going to get a divorce. It was truly a sad moment for both Mickey and Wynn, to realize that they would no longer be spending time together.

By 1935 Nell enrolled her son in a military school in Culver City, California. It was a convenient location for him since it was also close to the MGM studios where Mickey was now regularly working. It was however Mickey's intention to be a normal teenager, so it wasn't long afterwards that he enrolled in Fairfax High School. However, because of his commitment to MGM, it soon became apparent that he needed to attend a school that understood and supported students involved in film production. Thus, he enrolled in the Little Red Schoolhouse, a school created to meet these requirements.

In 1937, the MGM movie, *A Family Affair*, was released staring the young actor as Andy Hardy. The movie was an instant success, and led to the release of nearly twenty other Andy Hardy films. The young actor also starred in 1938 with Spencer Tracy in one of his most proclaimed films: *Boys Town*.

Meanwhile, the young actor became great friends with Judy Garland during the late thirties and early 1940s. They both appeared in a number of films together. In one such film, *Babes in Arms,* (released in 1939), Mickey received a nomination for Best Actor.

In 1944, Rooney was to star in the film, *National Velvet*, which also featured another young actress, Elizabeth Taylor. It was later during that same year when Mickey was inducted into the U.S. Army. For the next two years, his duties included entertaining troops overseas and acting as a radio announcer and entertainer on the American Forces Network. His mission was to boost the morale of the thousands of U.S. soldiers who were abroad during World War II.

While Mickey had a number of film and television successes during the decade of the 1950s, it appeared that his fame had declined from his success in the late '30s and the 1940s. Mickey, now in his 30s, managed to retain his popularity in a number of ways.

The decade of 1950 started out for the actor finding out that his father died on March 13th, and was buried in Forrest Lawn. However, soon after receiving this news, he won a lead part in the movie *The Fireball* starring Marilyn Monroe (released in 1950) and the 1954's The Bridges of Toko-Ri (starring Grace Kelley). Mickey also starred in a number of television shows as well. One such show featured the young man in thirty-two episodes.

Unfortunately, Mickey also found himself in difficult situations regarding his personal life. At the age of twenty-one he married his first wife, actress Ava Gardner. The marriage led to divorce only one year later. This trend repeated itself with four more failed marriages over the next twenty-three years. With his obvious personal problems, and a number of children to support, it was not surprising that in 1962, the forty-two year old actor filed for bankruptcy.

In his book, *Life Is Too Short*, Mickey clearly exposed one of the weaknesses in his life. He admitted that one well known actor friend took him to a local brothel near Santa Monica Blvd. He knew other Hollywood actors who were struggling with this addiction as well.

In the seventies the actor, now in his fifties, found success again with the release of the movie *The Adventures of the Black Stallion*. By 1979, he "made his Broadway musical debut in the acclaimed stage play, *Sugar Babies*."(7) The show would be featured on Broadway for some time with over 1,200 performances in New York. The musical would continue well into the 1980s when the performing artists including Mickey would continue playing in the show as it toured for five more years.

Rooney recounted in a number of interviews (both in print and on video) when he, during later in the 1980s, had an incredible visitation from God. It was a life changing moment for Mickey Rooney. According to an interview he did in 1995 with Kira Albin: Rooney was in a Lake Tahoe coffee shop for breakfast when he "was greeted by a busboy who with 'blond curls, a white–rose complexion, and shining teeth.' When the man called his name, Rooney started to stand, thinking he had a telephone call. But the busboy leaned toward him and whispered in his ear, 'Mr. Rooney, Jesus Christ loves you very much.' Then he left. Minutes later, Rooney looked for the busboy, but nobody knew of one who met Rooney's description and he was nowhere to be found." (8)

Mickey was never raised in a religious home and obviously this experience, as he would later testify, was a moment in time that had a profound effect on his life. Initially he became involved with the Church of Religious Science. However, he eventually moved away from that church and embraced evangelical Christianity.

The actor, now in his seventies, made a change for the better. He stayed with his eighth wife, Jan, for thirty-four years. However, they did separate during the last two years of his life. Suspecting that his age could have been a factor, he sold his home for over $1 million and gave much of the proceeds to his wife. It is Interesting that his marriage to Jan was longer than all his seven previous marriages combined and on the eventual day of his death (in 2014) he was still officially married.

By the year 2000 Mickey would also overcome his previous addiction to sleeping pills. He also became a fan of the Christian TV show: the 700 Club and its founder, Pat Robertson. Obviously his new yearnings towards Christ and His word (the Bible) encouraged the eighty year old actor's growth in his faith. Mickey's oldest son had also become a born-again Christian and was involved in the evangelical community in California. It's probably easy to assume that his oldest son also had a positive influence on Mickey and his following of Christ.

Mickey recounted after his angelic visitation in the coffee shop by saying that "if you go with God and with Jesus Christ as your personal Savior, and leave your troubles and everything with God, everything will work out for you"(9). Mickey freely admitted his many failings in the past. He was resolved to deal with some of his own personal issues and knew that the God of the Bible he was now serving was fully willing to forgive him of his sins.

Christ died on the cross for our sins and rose from the dead three days later. Christ's incredible sacrifice was witnessed by hundreds of his followers, some of whom would later die for their faith. Clearly Mickey recognized this and decided that he would no longer serve himself but would now serve the God of Heaven and Earth.

Over the course of the last years of his life Mickey occasionally pursued opportunities to appear in film. He loved to perform, and enjoyed working in his profession. This is not surprising since he acted in over 300 films during his lifetime. However, he now realized that was important for him to tell others about the gospel message of Christ.

Towards the end of Mickey's life, he was interviewed a number of times about his new found faith. It was a wonderful opportunity for him to share his faith in God. He knew from personal experience that the message of the cross would go a long way to change lives for the better. (Even today you can still find the video versions of these interviews on the internet).

On one such occasion Mickey encouraged parents to share their faith with their sons and daughters. By now the ninety year old recognized the importance of that message. He had nine children and two stepchildren who were obviously now grown up.

In a recorded message Mickey Rooney shared with his audience that: "You should take your children to church and teach them about Jesus Christ and about God, who makes the sun shine and the moon glow and gives us so many blessings…" (10)

Sadly, at the time of his death he had very little money to give his children due primarily to his bad choices from his past (i.e. gambling, and numerous divorces).

But what Mickey did leave them along with all his fans as well as millions across America is this clear message that Christ is the answer!

As one of the last surviving actors of Hollywood's classic era, it is a blessing that Mickey Rooney discovered the love of Christ and the message of salvation which can be clearly found in the Bible. With Mickey's dramatic touch from God, it is hoped that more people will come to discover the simple message from the book of John in the New Testament in the Bible:

> "For God so loved the world, that He gave His only begotten Son, that whosoever believes in Him should not perish but have ever lasting life". (John 3:16)

Mickey Rooney (courtesy of TCM movies)

Mickey Rooney star on Hollywood Blvd, Los Angeles

Melrose Hall, Linfield College, McMinnville, OR.

Chapter 8

Linfield College During The Early 1970s – Such A Time As This!

It was an extraordinary time at the 100+ year old college. During the early 1970s there was a wave of Christian revival called the Jesus Movement. It began in the 1960's on the west coast of California and spread throughout America, even touching other continents. Linfield College, as other colleges was impacted by this movement. In February of 1972, even the college newspaper, Linews, devoted a special addition of the campus' newspaper to The Jesus Revolution. Professors such as Gordon Frazee and Joseph Ban supported and encouraged students on campus in their new Christian faith.

Linfield was originally established in 1858. It was first charted as The Baptist College of McMinnville, and later the college was renamed McMinnville College. In 1922, the college was again given a new name: Linfield College. This change took place after Frances Eleanor Ross Linfield bestowed a substantial gift to the school in honor of her deceased husband, the Reverend George Linfield. Years later, Linfield College Professor Jonas Jonasson commented on Frances' gift by saying: "Mrs. Linfield's dual purpose in making the gift … was to perpetuate the name, scholarly attainments and

Christian influence of her late husband … and to promote the cause of Christian education." (1) Jonas Jonasson was a history professor at the college for many years, before retiring in 1970.

During the early 1970s there was a chapter of Campus Crusade for Christ (CCC) on campus. Linfield's Class of '71 graduate Dave Tillstrom was instrumental in forming that chapter. During the summer of 1970 Tillstrom attended a conference that was held by Campus Crusade in Arrowhead Springs, CA, where Dave learned how to share his faith in Jesus Christ. (2)

As Dave would later recall, "We took the school directory and shared the gospel to every fraternity and every sports team on campus… the results were astonishing. So many responded and grew in the Lord. So many were coming to the Lord that we had weekly meetings called College Life … One day one of the Linfield Board of Directors contacted me and asked if I would share with the board my testimony and what was going on campus … what a thrill and opportunity!" (2a)

The Campus Crusade chapter continued to share and spread the gospel of Christ around the college campus. By the end of spring semester in 1971,Tillstrom had graduated and Ron Verdoorn (class of '72) took over the reins of CCC on campus. According to a February 1972 edition of the college's newspaper, Campus Crusade for Christ was growing rapidly in popularity among the students.

One of Verdoorn's friends and basketball teammates was Dave Lower. He transferred to Linfield in the 1970's. One evening Ron asked Dave to join some friends in a meeting that was sponsored by Campus Crusade for Christ. It was through that initial social event that Ron became involved in their Bible study. Looking back on that time, Ron would later say that "the three years at Linfield gave me some solid growth in my spiritual journey through life. It gave me a foundation that God is still continuing to build in my life." (3)

Similar events occurred throughout the college during those days. Students would share their faith with their friends and fellow dorm mates. Back then, it was easy to access and share with fellow students who lived together in dorms on campus.

Through friendships and school events, God was able to touch a variety of students. One such student was local resident, Charmaine (Sanders) Klein. She had dedicated her life to Christ at age twelve while attending the First Christian Church in Tillamook. She vividly remembers surrendering her heart to Christ and experienced a peace that she remembers to this day. (4)

Charmaine's family later moved from Tillamook to McMinnville, Oregon. During her teenage years, Charmaine had a Christian mentor, Hanni Kock, who loved the Lord and was someone Charmaine could emulate (4a). After graduating from McMinnville High School, Charmaine began attending Linfield in 1970 during the fall semester.

As a freshman she attended Campus Crusade for Christ meetings. At an unrelated weekend retreat she met Larry Allen, who was a junior Linfield student at the time. It was there where she shared her faith with him and he accepted Christ. (4a) Under the urgings of the Holy Spirit, Larry felt compelled to share his new faith with others including a former New Dorm resident of his, Lee Lambert. During one February night in 1971 Larry read the Campus Crusade for Christ's Four Spiritual Laws Bible tract to Lee who, in his Hewitt Hall dorm room that evening, accepted Christ as his Lord and Savior.

Another Hewitt Hall dorm resident was also touched by the Holy Spirit not long after. His name was Steve Schrater. One evening a fellow dorm resident shared the Campus Crusade for Christ booklet with Steve too. Steve enthusiastically received the good news from the Christian tract and made the decision to commit his life to Christ. Within four months the college freshman traveled to Lolita, California where he would live at Lighthouse Ranch, a Christian commune.

Lighthouse Ranch was operated by Gospel Outreach and led by Senior Pastor Jim Durkin. Over time Steve became heavily involved in full time ministry, eventually becoming a pastor. Over the next 14+ years Steve reached out to a multitude of young people sharing with them the Good News of Jesus Christ. His efforts along with others from the Lighthouse Ranch ministry resulted in many young people being delivered from drugs and other addictions so they could now follow Christ as their Savior and Lord. Ultimately, the young former Linfield student made a significant difference in numerous lives during this time period.

Greg Herdon was also a Linfield student during this time period. During this time, he was a resident of Mac Hall and later Hewitt Hall on campus. Greg had a positive influence on his friend's lives. After fellow 3rd floor Hewitt Hall resident Lee accepted Christ in February of 1971, Greg mentored Lee, as a new follower of Christ. Greg would later become a minister. Now retired, Rev. Herdon most recently served as senior pastor for the St. James AME church in Erie, Penn. Prior to that, Reverend Herdon was appointed to a number of ministry positions in the AME district in Pennsylvania in which he served.

It was also during the early '70s when Linfield student Mike Hanna got involved with the school's local chapter of the Fellowship of Christian Athletes. FCA is a national organization centered on the Christian interaction of young athletes. (5)

During his freshman year Mike and his dorm roommate Mike Mattox had come to know the Lord the year before and wanted to help lead others in making their own decisions regarding their relationship with God. Mike would find Linfield's chapter of the Fellowship of Christian Athletes to be very accommodating in fulfilling its purpose.

Mike saw the early '70s as an interesting time as co-ed dorms were starting to open up and college students were no longer required to attend the school's weekly chapel service. (6) Mike would later recollect that he was proud that the weekly (Fellowship of Christian Athletes) meetings became a safe haven for those who wanted to grow in their faith and learn more about having a personal relationship with their Lord. (6a) Mike would later attribute his success during those years to his personal relationship with the Lord and his commitment to His word.

There were other dorm residents around the college who were touched by God and would eventually become involved in church ministries in various capacities. Some of these former students included former Hewitt Hall and former New Dorm resident John Parrot. Jon would later become a Christian missionary in Mexico. After that he served as an assistant for his church in Washington State.

Dillon Hall, located in the center of the campus on Linfield Avenue, was the school's cafeteria. It was inside Dillon Hall where Christian students had the opportunity to share their faith at their literature table. Dave Kuykendall and others including his future wife, Barbara, took advantage of their table to pass out Christian literature to students who showed interest in following Christ. Dave and his friends would also help students by answering questions that they might have had about the Christian faith.

Dave Kuykendall enrolled as a freshman at Linfield College in the fall of 1969. At the time, he considered himself as a nominal Christian who attended a church not known for sharing their faith. At that time, he conceded that he didn't have a prayer life and didn't read his Bible. In his firsts two semesters at Linfield, Dave was also known for his social action against the Vietnam War.

During the next college year Dave transferred to the University of Colorado. It wasn't long after that when he decided to transfer back to Linfield. As Dave would later concede "this time I found Linfield to be a different place. It seemed like the Jesus People movement has reached Linfield (and had) brought a spiritual fervor to the campus. I myself (became) … a baptized, Bible reading and praying Christian with a heart of sharing the gospel… I rejoiced to be involved in a completely rejuvenated Christian Student Union, now housed in what had previously been the most notorious fraternity house ... By the time that semester was over, there was a student-led weekly Bible study being conducted in every single dormitory on campus." (7)

David also noted that one of the highlights of his second time at Linfield was meeting his future wife, Barbara Godfrey. Dave fondly recollected that by saying that he was "approaching our 50th college reunion, and looking back with amazement at how God could transform people's lives in His great plan." (7a)

It was also during the early '70s when Frank and Adina Friesen were directed by God to move to the northwest U.S. from their home in Manitoba, Canada. As they drove through the town of McMinnville, Oregon they felt that the Lord was directing them to live there. Initially Frank rented a house for his their family of five near downtown McMinnville. It wasn't too long thereafter that Frank procured employment in the janitorial services department of the college.

Eventually the couple purchased a home directly across from Linfield's football field. Adina and Frank found the location ideal for their weekly Bible study and prayer meetings.

It was also during one Saturday night during the fall of 1971 when Linfield sophomore student Lori Smith knocked on fellow student Bob Prouty's door who, at the time, was also a resident of Larsell Hall. Lori asked Bob if his roommate was going to be at the Bible study at the Friesen's home. Since Bob's roommate wasn't there at the time, Lori asked (Bob) if he wanted to go instead. Bob responded by saying he was studying that night. Lori replied by saying: "Come on Bob, it is Saturday night. It is time to take a break." (8)

Bob would later remember this time by saying: "I reluctantly went along. I knew most of the people there. There were friends of my roommate and we often ate together at the college cafeteria."

Bob recalled his experience that night by saying: "This meeting was unlike anything I have experienced … People were talking about how Jesus was changing their lives. One person shared how 'Jesus had given them the power to flush all their drugs down the toilet.' I was impressed. Near the end of the meeting we formed a prayer circle and someone said 'There is one person in this circle who is not a Christian yet.' I knew who he meant… me. Somehow I knew that Jesus Christ had a right to direct my life because I was not letting him … So I said out loud, 'Jesus take control.' (8)

Bob continued by recalling that "Jesus began to change my life. My parents noticed it when I signed up for a typing class, something I avoided during high school. This is a skill I use every day as I write computer programs and content for the internet. I also had a great hunger to read the Bible to see what Jesus had done for me."(8)

As a new believer in Christ, Bob vividly remembers his experience by saying: "Soon after I became a follower of Jesus my roommate kicked me out and I moved to another dorm room. My roommate was an atheist. He spent the rest of the year trying to convince me that God does not exist. When I had doubts or questions, I would ride my bike to the Friesen home and share these with Mrs. Friesen. Her approach was always the same: have some tea, let me listen, lets pray. During prayer we had been in the presence of God and He washed away my doubts". (8)

Bob concluded by saying: "I've been a missionary with Campus Crusade for Christ for the past 40+ years, serving most of that time in Sydney, Australia. Sometimes I shudder to think what might have happened if Lori had not asked me to go to the Bible study that Saturday night or if I had said no to her invitation. I am grateful for the path Jesus has led me on and look forward to the future." (8)

Frank and Adina Friesen's prayer meetings were to also have a positive influence on a number of Linfield students and other McMinnville residents as well. Nick Burt was a local resident who attended the Friesen's prayer meetings. He would later attend Christ for the Nations Institute in Dallas, Texas. Nick and his future wife, Mary Cay, met at the Dallas school. "The two founded China Passage and traveled several times per year to remote areas of China and Tibet where they preached Christian beliefs and set up schools to educate underground churches" (9)

The Friesen's younger daughter Chris and her brother, Warren went to McMinnville High school during the '70s. Chris, Warren and Arlene, (their older sister), were all to become involved in Christian ministry over the years.

It was also during this time when some other former students of the local high school in McMinnville, attended the Friesen's weekly Bible and prayer meetings. They included local resident Tim McGill. Looking back now, Tim admitted that in late February to early March in 1972 his life "had begun to spin out of control because of alcohol and drug abuse." In the absence of any prom-ising future or perceived positive direction in life, he decided to revisit the possibility that the God of the Bible could actually exist." (10) It was over the course of the next several months when Tim realized that he could either continue his current life style or get to know the loving God of the Bible. The Bible studies and prayer meetings at the Friesen household would also speak to Tim's heart. Through them, God demonstrated His love to Tim.

Over the course of the next few months, Tim left his home in Oregon and moved to Dallas, Texas where he attended Christ for the Nations Institute. Tim's attendance at that Bible school not only had a positive influence on his life, but It was there where he also met his future wife, Cindy Lou Woody. Since that time, Tim and Cindy have pastored four churches in Oregon and Utah. Currently Tim resides near Ft. Worth, Texas where they, once a week, lead an Encounter Service, at the Open Door Church in Burleson, Texas.

It was also during the early '70s that a number of students reg-ularly drove an hour north to attend the Friday night service at the

Maranatha Church in Portland. The church was headed by Senior Pastor Wendell Wallace. As a very inspirational minister, he pastored a very influential inter-racial church in Portland, Oregon. Their music and choir was led by Rev. Richard Probasco. That weekly Friday night service touched the hearts of many Linfield students as well as their entire congregation. Even today Rev. Probasco is still in the ministry as he leads the New Song Church, another popular church located in the Portland community.

Back then, Rick Loomis was a Linfield student who also was positively affected by the college's Christian influence. As someone who had recently experienced a life changing encounter with Christ at the Prince of Peace coffee house in Portland, Oregon (11), Rick decided to open a Christian coffee house on the campus.

Along with other friends, Rick secured a location that was formerly occupied by a fraternity house. The coffee house was the scene of numerous Christian events during its 1 ½ year run. As Rick later recalled, the house was "open on Friday and Saturday nights. There was often live music from Christian bands... clearly, the workings of the Holy Spirit was evident back then..." (11)

Rick Loomis was also thankful for the spiritual encouragement he received from Frank and Adina Friesen during their weekly Bible studies and prayer meetings. He additionally cites the spiritual encouragement he received from Linfield's Professor Frazee. Rick would later receive his Ph.D. in theology degree in 2001 from Fuller Seminary in Pasadena, CA.

By early May of 1972, there were at least 75 Linfield Christian students who had a prayer meeting on the lawn in front of Dillon Hall. At that time, Dillon Hall was located in the center of campus (on Linfield Avenue) and was and still is the main cafeteria for the college. The prayer meeting in front of Dillon effectively acted as the starting point for the students Walk for Christ that day. The students involved shared their faith in Christ with local residents as they walked to the downtown section of McMinnville, by passing out Four Spiritual Laws tracts. A number of other Linfield students then traveled up to Portland. The group concluded their travel at the South Park Blocks near Portland State University at 5pm on Saturday afternoon. (12)

As reported in an article in *the Oregonian* (Portland's main newspaper) some of these other Christian students from the college used the Walk for Christ to obtain sponsorship to fund their attendance to the Explo '72 event in Texas. Explo was a Christian conference on evangelism which took place in Dallas a month later. The walkathon had the support of a number of well-known churches in the city of Portland as well as the surrounding counties in Oregon.

God touched the lives of many Linfield College students during the 1970s. Clearly, the college years are a pivotal time for many young people when decisions are made and patterns form that often have a long time effect on college students. This truly demonstrates how important it is today for followers of Christ to reach out to college age students on campuses all over the country.

If for any reason a believer cannot do this, it is still important for Christians to support ministries that reach out to college students or, in the very least, pray for their success. America's future depends on it !

Ron Verdoorn

Jon
Parrott

Greg
Herndon

Dave Kuykendall raps with students about Jesus (courtesy: Linews)

Praise Chapel, formerly Assembly of God church, McMinnville, OR.

Rev. Richard Probasco, New Song Church, Portland, OR. & former Music Minister for Maranaha Church of God

Maranatha Church's hall where Fri. Night services were once held

Maranatha Church of God, Portland, OR. – Main entry

Rick Loomis, Linfield College – class of '74

Frank and Adina Friesen (taken in McMinnville, Oregon)

"An evening at the CSU coffeehouse" (courtesy of Oak Leaves '72)

Chapter 9

How Reading The Bible Transformed A Young Detroit Boy & Led Him To Serving God Through-Out His Life

Adlai Mack was born in Harper Hospital in Michigan on February 24th, 1954. Adlai grew up in a Christian home. His parents, Albert and Nina were members of the Plymouth Congressional Church in their hometown in Detroit, Michigan.

From the age of four, Adlai's 9 year old sister, Zaneta, regularly read the family Bible to him. At an early age, the young boy knew that he would never need another savior in his life other than the Lord Jesus Christ. When Adlai was 13, he fully comprehended the gospel message outlined in the Bible, and dedicated his life to God. He also had a decisive encounter with the Holy Spirit as he would later recall when "the Spirit of God fell on" him. (1)

Two more children were born to the Mack family. Valinda was born in 1956, and the youngest, Regina, was born in 1961. During his teens, Adlai would share the gospel with his sisters resulting in both of them deciding to commit their lives to Christ.

During the early 1960's Adlai started having difficulties with bullies at school. At the same time in Detroit, a variety of negative social issues and increased crime in general resulted in neighborhoods becoming dangerous. Gangs began to run rampant in many local communities throughout the once safe city of Detroit, Michigan.

Despite all this turmoil in his young life, Adlai found comfort in the Bible and memorizing scripture. Adlai noticed that this strategy helped him deal with the bullying at school. The Holy Spirit also became an important source of guidance, protection and direction to him in his life.

Albert, his father, owned a barber shop in the city called the Chesterfield Barber Shop. Albert was also a well-respected leader in the black community. By the time he was in middle school Adlai was able to work part time in his father's business as a shoeshine boy. By 1960, his mother began working for the Pittsburg Courier newspaper. Over time her career was to advance to the point where she was to be assigned to the position of General Manager for the weekly newspaper.

As a young 13 year old teenage boy, Adlai was stunned one day when he saw his father hit his mother. He suspected that Albert was intoxicated, yet the incident made him so angry that he started entertaining thoughts of killing his father. Adlai's memorization of Bible verses paid off, reminding him of the Ten Commandments verse 'Thou shalt not kill.' Adlai realized that any thoughts he had of murder were unacceptable to his loving God.

From 1968 to 1972 Adlai attended Samuel Mumford High School. There he played on the school's football team. He also learned how to defend himself by practicing tae kwon do. With the encouragement of Katie, one of his mother's close friends, Adlai applied to Princeton University and would soon thereafter be accepted to attend the prestigious college.

In the spring of 1972 the high school senior gave the class graduation speech before a packed audience. He would also take the opportunity to insert the gospel message in his speech as well. Overall his message that day was overwhelmingly received by the audience, which was a foreshadowing of the young man's future career.

Always drawn to sharing the gospel, Adlai had posted a notice at the YMCA to find others who were interested in forming a bible study. Adlai was contacted by a man offering his local address as a place to meet. As Adlai entered the building, he knew something was wrong. The man was there, along with eight other men. As it turned out all of them were gang members who had the intention of raping the 18 year old high school graduate.

Immediately Adlai started praying to his Heavenly Father. He knew he was in trouble. He felt the Holy Spirit telling him to treat this incident as if he was playing tackle football. He put his head down and quickly dashed to the door, plunging into anyone who tried to stop him.

Much like a running back would do with a defender, he ran through three doors. He ran up the stairs and headed outside. When he was close to his car he literally leaped into the open convertible. He landed on the driver's seat and his keys were suddenly in his hand. Fortunately, the car started right away and he raced for home as he was still being chased by the gang members. Clearly, Adlai was very thankful to his Heavenly Father that he had escaped the gang members that day.

In the fall of '72, the 18 year young man began attending Princeton University. During his freshman year Adlai helped form the Alpha Omega Christian Fellowship, a spirit filled fellowship "with signs and wonders", on campus. The Christian Fellowship consisted of around 25 students along with graduate students and town residents. During the next few years, the fellowship would minister to around 4,500 Princeton students reaching out to them on campus and going door to door to their dormitories on campus. Additionally members of the ministry on weekends and holidays would also reach out to communities in nearby states (New York, Virginia, Michigan and Florida) which included passing out over 25,000 tracts to non-believers.

Adlai majored in history, and by June of 1976, his parents would join him at his college graduation ceremony at Princeton University that month. (2)

Adlai would then move back to Detroit after he graduated from college. That summer, the Plymouth Congregational Church gave the young man a summer job as their Assistant Director of their 'Summer Camp for Kids'. Adlai also applied for and was accepted to the Gordon Conwell Seminary in Massachusetts. He attended the seminary for 3 years, graduating in the spring of 1979.

At the Seminary Adlai met his future wife, Sandra Scribner. They married at the West Peabody Church on May 27, 1978. The couple settled in Gloucester, MA while he continued his education at the Seminary. It was also during this time when Adlai expressed interest in becoming a missionary. Accordingly, he applied to be a missionary with several governmental agencies from China and Nigeria. Subsequently, he was turned down by both of these countries. Adlai and his wife were also both active with three evangelistic teams during his time while in seminary school. During this time Sandra would go on a short term missions trip to Japan.

After graduating from seminary school, Adlai and Sandra returned to his old church in Detroit where Adlai was ordained as a minister. With his impressive resume, he applied for a number of pastoral positions in churches across the country (more successfully in the states of Florida, Hawaii and California.)

It was in California where the young pastor discovered a small church when he "had a vision concerning Christian Fellowship Church." (3) The church was located on Kelton Road in San Diego. At the time of this new assignment, the church met in their child care facility because their main building had been destroyed in the late '60s by a fire. Apparently the Christian Fellowship church had no fire insurance for the building, which explains why a new church building had not yet replaced the old structure.

Over the course of the next few years Adlai watched the church attendance and church donations increase by over 400%. His church became one of the top 6 revitalized churches from this denomination in the country. Between 1983 and 1984 the main sanctuary of the church was rebuilt.

Due to the success of his new church, Adlai was able to go on speaking engagements to many churches throughout the country. The religious group, Biblical Witness Fellowship, financed this endeavor.

Sadly the Bishop who had oversight over the Christian Fellowship Church denomination mandated several new policies that would ultimately affect Rev. Mack's church. The Bishop wanted the church to defend the practice of homosexually as well as support the abortion of babies in the womb. The church's leaders were also directed to agree with the practice of assisted suicide and ignore the fallacies of communism.

Being a firm follower of the God of the Bible, Rev. Mack could not accept these new precepts which clearly contradicted the Bible. Unable to conform to these new dictates, Adlai resigned from the position of church pastor on September 13 1984. He had served as lead pastor of the Christian Fellowship Church for exactly 5 years.

While the young pastor was ministering around the country, as one of the leaders of Biblical Witness Fellowship, he had a dream one night about opening a house church. A house church is "an evangelical Christian congregation independent of traditional denominations and mainly or originally meeting in the private homes of its members" (dictionary). With the encouragement of over 50 of his former church members, he opened a local house church. Due to community zoning regulations the home church, initially located at a house in San Diego, was moved to Gompers Secondary School in S.E. San Diego. Within a year the church doubled from 50 to 100 members. Then over a period of the next 25 years Adlai founded the Christians United Church. This new church, over a period of time grew to 250 members and would move to various locations around San Diego ranging from

Mission Valley to Spring Valley and finally to its present location in S.E. San Diego.

It was also during the year 1973 when Adlai Mack would become actively involved in communicating to the public about the dangers of abortion. Adlai regularly stood in front of churches, on university lawns and on public sidewalks preaching about the evils of abortion. He also informed the public about the millions of babies who had lost their lives at abortion clinics across the country.

Initially Adlai became aware of the dangers of the abortion industry during the year (1973) when it was legalized in the now famous Supreme Court case: Roe vs. Wade. On this issue he was positively influenced by Professor Paul Ramsey who also taught Christian Ethics at Princeton University.

Between 1981 and 2017 Reverend Mack along with a number of his pro-life friends were actively involved in providing public side-walk counseling in front of abortion clinics to women and men around Southern California. He made signs, would preach and would even show movies teaching folks about the horrors of abortion. Ultimately Adlai influenced over 2,000 at risk women to save their babies from the abortion clinics. He would also adopt 2 children who were once at risk of being aborted. Over a period of almost 20 years, Adlai and a number of his friends were responsible for helping to close down eighteen such clinics. Further, his actions would also help to persuade a number of abortionists to leave the industry.

Not many people realize that Planned Parenthood's founder, Margaret Sanger, had a notorious reputation. Her well documented quotes include: "The most merciful thing that the large family does to one of its infant members is to kill it."(This quote is from Margaret Sanger's book: Woman and the New Race, Chapter. 5 - "The Wickedness of Large Families"). In yet another quote Sanger clearly demonstrates her racist attitude: "We don't want the word to go out that we want to exterminate the Negro population." (Letter to Dr. Clarence J. Gamble 12/10/1939 - pg. 2 Libex.smith.edu/ omeka...)

In October of 2007 Adlai traveled to Washington D.C. to protest a recent legal decision in front of the Supreme Court which mandated the removal of a Ten Commandments plaque in the state of Alabama. Judge Moore from Alabama was also at the rally which included over 300 people in attendance. At the rally Rev. Mack spoke, informing the people about the danger of the federal government's infringement of freedom of speech and religion. (4)

By later that day, the attendees increased to over 1500 people, and were to participate in a prayer vigil that evening. Apparently (according to Rev. Mack) it was unlawful at that time to have a Bible at that particular public park area in Washington D.C. (near the Supreme Court). It was also at that same location when a number of military dressed U.S. Marshals were present.

The U.S. Marshals, who were on the scene decided to take action by violently removing all the participants who had Bibles in their possession. They held them at gunpoint. As it turned out Adlai's whole worship team were "arrested … for holding Bibles in their hands." (4) Adlai and others would later stay that day until the rally detainees were all finally released. After each of the detainees where accounted for, Adlai decided to head back to California.

Adlai and his wife Sandra have had three children who are now fully grown. Their first child was named John, was born in 1980 at the Paradise Valley Hospital in National City. Rebekah was born in 1984 and their third child, Joanna Mack, was born in 1986.

All three of their kids are now successfully pursuing their occupations. John Mack lives in Long Beach, CA. and is an expert mechanical engineer who works for Raytheon Corporation where is highly regarded in his field. Rebekah lives in Lemon Grove, CA. and is as a school teacher & assistant director at the school where she works. Joanna lives in St. Louis, MO. and worked in the medical field. She is now a dispatcher for Tri-Nation.

Adlai and Sandra are proud of their son and two daughters. They enjoy the times they can spend camping together. Adlai is also involved in helping the homeless and poor population in his community by his allegiance with the S.E. Minstrel Alliance. Rev. Mack is still active in the ministry as the pastor of his own local church, Christians United, in southeast San Diego. Just like many pastors from around the country, he continues to encourage folks in their faith by his sermons and the Bible studies he gives each week.

Rev. Adlai Mack understands the importance of being faithful to God. As you can see by Adlai's story, he continues to depend on prayer to his loving God in order to get New Testament heavenly guidance for his life.

I'm sure if you care to request prayer for you or your family or friends, Adlai will be glad to talk to you. Reverend Mack, Pastor of Christians United Church in San Diego, can be reached at (619) 370-9616.

Chapter 10

Ann B. Davis: Her Story

A nn Bradford Davis, along with twin sister Harriet, was born to
Cassius and Marguerite Davis on May 3rd, 1926. The family
lived in Schenectady, New York. After three years the Davis family,
along with older siblings Evans and Elizabeth, moved to the state of
Pennsylvania. Ann eventually graduated from Strong Vincent High
School in Erie, Pennsylvania. (1)

During the latter part of high school, Ann decided to enroll in the
University of Michigan. Originally Ann was drawn to the field of med-
icine and planned to steer her future career in that direction. However,
after viewing several theatrical performances, she switched her major
to Drama. Ann graduated from the University of Michigan in 1948.

Ann spent the next five years honing her skills in acting by performing in various theaters and touring in musicals. Ultimately, Ann
relocated to Porterville, California in order to work in the Barn Theater,
a popular venue in that community. Her move to California would
eventually lead to her securing her first roles in film, television and
even television advertising.

Initially some of these first appearances were unaccredited.
However, it soon became evident that the young actress was consumed

with her pursuit of becoming a successful actress. Her commitment was absolute, even at the expense of friendships and dating.

By 1955 Ann was selected as the supporting actress in the weekly television broadcast, *The Bob Cummings Show*. The show was syndicated on both NBC and CBS television Networks where Ann was featured in 159 episodes. Ms. Davis was also nominated for an Emmy as best-supporting actress for one of the seasons during the years that the show was broadcast, from 1955 to 1959.

Obviously after the airing of this popular '50s television show Ann had established herself as a well-recognized actress. She also appeared in 29 episodes of the John Forsythe television show from 1965 to 1969, not to mention the numerous single appearances she made on various game shows, films, and television interviews. (1)

Later, the actress (now in her 40s), secured a starring role in the popular TV show: *The Brady Bunch*. The show featured six children (actors Barry Williams, Christopher Knight, Mike Lookinland and actresses Maureen McCormick, Eve Plumb and Susan Olsen) and their two made for TV parents (Florence Henderson & Robert Reed).

Ann Davis played the family's live-in maid and caretaker. The series was quite successful, running for five years (from 1969 to 1974). Later, this well-known TV show had a series of spin-off television episodes which included *The Brady Girls Get Married*, *A Very Brady Christmas* and others.

Over time Ann started questioning the direction that her life was taking. To quote an article by Gail Purath (from the Christian Woman's Fellowship): "During the success of the Brady Bunch, Miss Davis began to feel a real emptiness in her life. She had a lovely home in Hollywood and could afford to buy anything she wanted … She began to wonder 'What kind of greedy am I?' She couldn't imagine what was missing in her life."

The 48 year old actress soon realized that while she was successful in show business, there must be more to life than to being a successful television and film actress. She decided that she wanted to dedicate the rest of her life to God. Ann began attending Campus Crusade for Christ bible studies in order to educate herself about the Christian faith.

"In 1976, she shocked the world by semi-retiring from the acting business and became a born-again Christian. Davis then moved to an Episcopal community, even attending the Episcopal School for Ministry and joining a religious community in Denver, Colorado (later relocated near San Antonio, Texas)." (2)

Bishop Frey of the Episcopal Church in Denver (now retired) also exerted a positive influence on her life, encouraging Ann in her belief in God. According to the Christian Women's Fellowship, Ann's new dedication to Christ also helped her address her drinking problem.

During the next thirty odd years, Ann spent most of her time living in Episcopal Christian communities in Denver, Colorado and later in San Antonio, Texas. Housing in this community ranged from 9 to 24 people, all living together in the church community's building.

Ann spent several days a week preparing for each Bible study that she participated in at Helena's Church in Boerne, Texas, as well as singing in the church choir. In an article featured in *Web Pro News*, Ann noted that she spent a lot of time giving Christian witness all over the country to church groups. (3) Obviously this Christian testimony from a well-known actress had a positive effect on many. Ann was determined to impact as many people as she could with the salvation message of Christ. William Frey later recalled how Ann would give her testimony about how the Lord reawakened her. Her message of Christ's salvation in her life would also bless many of her fans as well. (4)

Ann's positive actions and dedication to following Christ clearly demonstrated that she understood the importance of sharing her faith. As the New Testament clearly teaches, it is important to spread the loving message of the Gospel around the world. Ann truly seemed to enjoy living a quiet but full life working with the Episcopal Church. (4) She was involved with her Christian faith up until the time of her passing.

On Saturday June 1st 2014, Ann's friends Bishop Bill and Barbara Frey received a phone call when Ann failed to show up at a scheduled hair appointment that morning. Concerned about their friend, they went to her room at the Episcopal community apartment and discovered that the former actress had fallen and hit her head in the bathroom. Ann was immediately taken to a nearby hospital in San Antonio, Texas. Sadly she never regained consciousness that day and died 24 hours later. Her Episcopal Christian community was struck with much grief after hearing the news of Ann's death. (4)

Considering the good health she enjoyed, Ann's friends were shocked by this sad turn of events. Nevertheless, Ann is in Heaven today and rejoicing with the many people she encouraged to follow Christ and serve Him as their Lord and Savior.

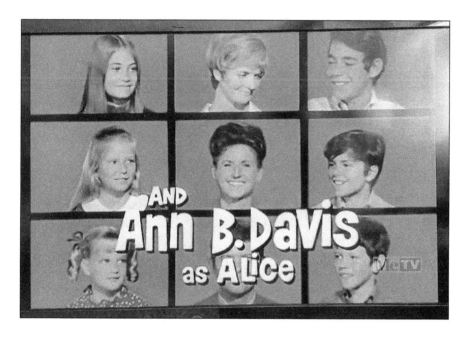

Caption: Ann B. Davis, *Brady Bunch* (courtesy of Metv television)

Caption: James Hartline, TV interview (courtesy of KUSI TV – San Diego)

Chapter 11

James Hartline's Dramatic Personal Transformation And Touch From God

J ames Hartline was born in the spring of1958, to Doug and Donna Hartline. Doug Sr. was a soldier in the United States Marines who fought during the Korean War in the early 1950s. In 1962 James' father retired from the Marine Corps reserves.

For the first ten years of James' life the young boy lived in Bakersfield, California. In 1969 after James graduated from 5th grade, his family moved to Chicago, Illinois. Sadly during those years, James would endure a variety of hardships as well as his exposure to pornography to a very young age. His family would later relocate to be closer to James' grandfather and other relatives as well

In 1971, James family moved again, this time to Carson City, Nevada. At the age of thirteen James faced the beginning of many challenges that were to occur in his lifetime. James was distressed by his relationship with his mother whom he "felt" was abusive to him.

James believed that the source of this abuse, according to James personal testimony was that his mother suffered from abuse herself. James suspected that this revelation explained her hostility towards him. (1)

James developed a pattern in life of running away in order to get away from this own personal hardships. By the age of 13, he "got up the courage to run away." He occasionally shoplifted which eventually got him in trouble with the law. At the age of fourteen James was sent to a children's home in Nevada. There, James excelled in academics but was marked poorly in conduct. His parents left him there and moved back to Bakersfield, CA.

In 1973 James was transferred to the Nevada Youth Training Center in Elko, Nevada. At age seventeen James resided in a half-way house known as *His Place* that was operated by the Assembly of God Church in Reno, Nevada.

One day, as the seventeen year old passed through a public park, a man picked him up and took him to a gay bar. Employees at the bar did not ask for James ID. The man treated James, who was touched by his generosity. This new acquaintance soon made his ulterior motive apparent when he took James, who was obviously a minor, to a gay bath house.

By the spring of 1976, James received his diploma from Reno High School. It was also during that summer when he stole money and ran off to San Francisco. Once there, he continued to be drawn into the gay lifestyle. While in the bay area James had to steal money so he could afford to live week to week in run-down hotel rooms.

As the fall of '76 approached, the eighteen year old traveled by bus back to Carson City, Nevada. James was soon arrested for breaking into a local business office. For this offense, he was sentenced to three years in prison, but ended up being released one year early. Initially James was assigned to the Nevada State Prison. After a few months there, James was transferred to the Nevada Correctional Center. By now James realized he was messed up both physically and mentally. (2)

As the head of the center's athletic department, Danny Nardico (also a former marine and professional boxer) tried to take the teenager under his wing. He realized that the young man was at risk of being brutalized by other correctional center residents there. James was thin and did not measure up physically to others in the Nevada Correctional Center. Danny knew that James would not be able to hold his own against a lot of tough guys, and was concerned for his personal safety.

By the middle of 1978, James completed his prison term in Nevada. He moved back to Oakland, California where he lived in a half-way house operated by homosexuals. It was at time period when an acquaintance introduced James to drugs. Right then James felt that God was telling him to leave the area. Drugs were a bad thing. After a relatively short period of time, James decided to travel to Hollywood, California, where he was again arrested … this time for a misdemeanor offense. James was placed into the Los Angeles County jail.

The young man was then transferred to the state of Nevada for what ended up being a new charge of possession of stolen property. It was decided by the court that James would serve another three year term (from 1979 to 1982) since he already had been convicted and served time on other charges in that state as well.

Fearful of re-entering Nevada's prison system, James became despondent. He felt depressed and hopeless. James was deeply troubled about the environment that he would now be required to live in. He couldn't identify with any of the other prisoners, and knew that being in prison again would only continue the downward spiral that his life had become. He also felt he was trapped in life, knowing he had no skills to offer anyone. Frustrated, James entertained suicidal thoughts about his failed life. He slashed his wrists in his first failed suicide attempt. Because of the suicide attempt, James was placed in the prison's psychiatric ward. It was also during this time when he was allowed to attend church services in the prison.

It wasn't too long after that when the authorities allowed James to be housed in a Christian dormitory. The dormitory allowed only Christian residents. Although his future dorm residents knew that James was coming from the psychiatric ward, he had now declared himself as a Christian. He also began to read his Bible regularly.

In 1982 James was offered parole while he was still living in the Christian dormitory. In order to get paroled he had to find a place to live. He had contacted his parents for help but they would not reach out to their twenty-four year old son. Ultimately he found a half-way house in Oakland and received parole. Unfortunately it wasn't too long after this that he found himself again among residents who were involved in the drug culture as well as the homosexual lifestyle.

James decided to move back to Hollywood and lived in a YMCA facility for four months. During this time he met a young man and they ended up moving to a youth hostel in the community of Ocean Beach in San Diego. James had only $600 cash in his possession. Unfortunately all his money was soon stolen by his new friend.

Since James had already made reservations to stay in a gay hostel for one week, he didn't know how to get the money to pay for his stay. Sadly, he returned to his old habit of burglary.

During the fall of '82 James was charged with breaking into someone's home and was subsequently arrested by undercover enforcement agents. James tried to commit suicide once more, this time in the California Rehabilitation Center. He was later sent to The California Men's Colony in San Luis Obispo, (SLO). He ended up serving a two year prison term from October of '82 to October of '84. Years later, James confessed that it bothered him to this day that during this time he reverted back to crime. (3)

After James was released from jail, he was paroled and lived in San Diego. While he did try to improve his behavior, James returned to his old pattern of stealing. Ultimately he was arrested, this time in 1985. From March of '85 to 1989, he served time in a variety of facilities from the San Diego County Jail to the Psych Unit to the California Men's Colony in San Luis Obispo, California.

After his release in 1989, the thirty-one year old again found himself in prison. His new seven year term of imprisonment included time where he would spend over a year in the San Diego County jail and close to six years in the California Men's Colony in SLO. James' time there also included treatment from the Atascadero State Hospital in San Luis Obispo. About a year before his prison terms expired, James contacted his grandfather Vernon Van Meir. James remembered a summer as a young boy when he lived with his grandparents and attended their local Lutheran church. In an effort to help his grandson, Vernon invited James to move in with him at his home in California, but this request was denied by the parole department.

On July 3rd, 1997 James moved back to San Diego County. His grandfather gave him some money which enabled him to survive. James reported to a parole officer in Chula Vista, a town located just south of downtown San Diego. Knowing that James was struggling again with drug use, the parole officer suggested that he attend AA meetings. James made arrangements to go to the local Salvation Army facility. It was also during this time when he again fell back into homosexuality.

By December of 1997, James (while on parole) discovered that he was infected with AIDS. His health became so impacted that he had to be treated at the UCSD Hospital in San Diego. James felt that this disease was the final nail in his coffin (4). He had come to a point in his life where he knew that he needed to be delivered and reconciled to his loving God and Savior Jesus Christ.

September of 2000 marked the end of James parole period. He now fully realized that his long internal struggle needed to end. James knew that his mind, emotions and will needed to be under the direction of His loving Lord God.

After the numerous personal trials and disappointments James experienced during his lifetime, he was now beginning to understand the importance of drawing close to God. He wanted to be free of the dark behavior and addictions he had succumbed to in the past.

During this period of great inroads, James was tempted by what he recognized as a demonic oppression to do drugs. He quickly learned from that experience that it was more important for him to have his will in the hands of his loving Heavenly Father than in the control of evil entities.

Upon reaching out to God in prayer, James realized that his desire to follow God far outweighed any desire to sin. He vowed to stop doing drugs and decided to give up the homosexual lifestyle.

James knew that it was spiritual warfare that he was in the midst of. He clearly understood that his past lifestyle of drugs, homosexuality and theft were contrary to the teachings of the Bible. He also understood from the Word that his will was often contrary to what God willed. James yearned to do just that: God's will. His changed heart brought about immediate results.

James started working at a local Goodwill Store. He also qualified for some government assistance due to past mental and disability issues. He even found a local church, (the Scott Memorial Baptist Church in North Park), that he initially attended. Over time, James became consumed with reading the Word and communing with his Heavenly Father. He was now truly a committed follower of his savior Jesus Christ.

It was also during the next decade that James Hartline began to publically expose some of the dangers of the homosexual lifestyle. He was acutely and personally aware of the obvious dangers as someone who had contracted AIDS. He started writing an email newsletter and a blog (www.jameshartlinereport.blogspot.com) entitled *The James Hartline Report* which is now posted on the internet.

With this convenient form of communication, he found a vehicle to express his new convictions and biblical stands. James believed it was important for him to tell others about the negative consequences of living the homosexual lifestyle from someone who had once personally experienced that lifestyle himself.

While the Bible views the homosexual lifestyle as sinful, today's society views it quite differently. Clearly, many Americans now are willing to accept the gay lifestyle as well as condone homosexual marriage.

By 2005, it was common for many local politicians and civic leaders around the country (including those in San Diego) to endorse

'Gay Pride' parades in their cities. As many people these days prefer to be 'politically correct', James spoke candidly about issues he felt the Lord was compelling him to address. He talked about his experiences as a former homosexual. He also addressed the importance of believers following Christ and sharing their faith with friends and neighbors.

Hartline later formed a group entitled *Not on My Watch* which regularly addressed members of the San Diego City Council on a variety of issues. He has also been interviewed on the 700 Club, the Trinity Broadcasting Network, KUSI television, the San Diego Reader publication, the American Family Radio Network, and The Paul McGuire Radio Show.

One hot political issue that James was involved in was the debate concerning the Mount Soledad Cross which was located on public property in La Jolla, California. A local atheist by the name of Phillip Paulson along with several of his lawyers led the charge to have the famous cross torn down because it was on federal land. They insisted that because of its location, this religious symbol was illegal. They made their point by reciting the constitutional clause involving the separation of church and state.

This is a common misinterpretation of the separation of church and state clause in the Constitution. The clause was added to protect the church from the state, not the other way around. What opponents of the cross ignored is that when the cross was erected (in the early 1950's) it was as a monument dedicated to fallen American soldiers from World War I, World War II and the Korean War. The monument adhered to the same tradition which public cemeteries held, namely crosses over grave sites to honor the dead.

James and his supporters opposed efforts to tear down the cross. This legal case went on for a number of years until the Mount Soledad Association purchased the twenty-nine foot cross and land for $1.4 million from the U.S. Defense Department in 2015. The cross still stands today.

Hartline's Christian activism continued. In 2008, he was involved in a local effort joined by fellow believers to inform the public (from the City Heights region of San Diego) about those who were struggling with poverty. Their 'March against Poverty' attracted a local school board member, Priscilla Schrebier. James organized the march which ultimately attracted over 100 residents including members of some local churches. They even spent time that day cleaning up neighborhoods and picking up trash.

Later that same year James ran for a seat on the San Diego City Council, only to lose his election in November of 2008. While James was well known in City Heights, he was running in a district that was considered to be the center of the gay community in San Diego County.

James quickly tackled another problem in the city. The porn industry had a number of locations (adult bookstores and strip clubs) which he viewed as having a negative influence in the community. He successfully applied pressure on city leaders to close down dozens of these locations that were in violation of existing City zoning regulations.

For these efforts, James received many physical threats of violence through phone calls, comments posted on line and even four physical assaults.

While James is still infected with AIDS, he is being successfully treated by a local doctor. In 2016 his doctor reported that he was healed from adrenal insufficiency, a condition in which the adrenal glands do not produce adequate amounts of steroid. In 2017, he was also healed of Hepatitis C. After hearing the good news from his doctor, James realized that his health was improving.

James' health has improved to the point to where he is now competing in half-marathon races. He feels more motivated than ever to continue his mission of sharing truth and his faith in Christ. James continues to post on the James Hartline Report which he started 15+years ago. James also has an instagram account (Instagram.com/ saintjameshartline) and youtube.com which you can view and connect with him too.

As in years past, James continues to strengthen his faith by regularly reading his Bible and praying to his loving God in Heaven. James' story is a powerful account of how our dear Lord waits patiently for us to return to Him. Although the path James chose was filled with troubles, in the end, James allowed the God of the universe to rescue him. As someone who enjoys sharing his faith, James hopes that with his story will help you find yourself in the arms of our loving Father too!

In the pages of the Bible, we can see that our loving God is there for us: "When he calls to me, I will answer him; I will be with him in trouble; I will rescue him and honor him. (Psalms 91:15) Clearly, we should fully realize that our Heavenly Father is always there for us too!

Chapter 12

Tribute To A Former College Roommate: John Parrott

I fondly remember the time during my freshman year (second semester) in college when John Parrott was my roommate at Linfield College in McMinnville, Oregon. I lost my previous roommate after my first semester (fall of 1968) when he decided to leave the college.

As my new roommate, John was a few years older than I. He was a friendly person and easy to get along with. Our dormitory was completed and built by the spring of 1968. It hadn't yet been officially named yet, thus the name 'New Dorm'. New Dorm was surrounded by three other men's dormitory housing units in the quad, (Hewitt Hall, Larsell & Anderson Hall), all of which were located just west of the college's football stadium.

John Parrott was born in Spokane, Washington in 1948. Tragically, he never knew his father because his father suffered a fatal accident during a military training flight which occurred when John was just two weeks old. Because of this circumstance and others, John and his mother, Jean, shared a close bond.

John graduated from Sealth High School in Seattle, Washington in 1966 and was accepted to attend Linfield College in McMInnville,

Oregon that fall. John had a lot of charisma and was well liked at the college, where he had a number of friends.

Larry Anderson, one of John' former dorm mates, recollected the memorable times he spend with John which included an automobile trip they took together to Seattle in John's 1963 Olds Star Fire (1).

I remember John's keen ability to repair and maintain his Oldsmobile. On the weekends John could be seen cruising around the town of McMinnville, picking up some beer, or visiting a pub in downtown McMinnville. John liked to drink during his early years, as did a number of young men at the college during that time.

I also remember how much John enjoyed the music of Johnny Cash. I fondly recollect the many times he would play Johnny's popular albums in our room.

One evening John has a difficult time going to sleep. He was annoyed by the light coming into our room that evening from an outside porch light from across the quad. John would then walk over to the closet and pulled out a rifle. He then slot out the light bulb with one quick pull of the trigger. It was a hilarious episode that I still remember to this day.

By the fall of '69, John was relocated to another dorm. Since we were now in different dormitories and were in different classes, John and I didn't see much of each other after that semester.

After going to Linfield for four years, John decided to return to Seattle. He continued to drink, yet still maintained a close relationship with his mother, whose strong faith in Christ left a positive impact on her son. "After a few years without direction John found Jesus Christ as his Lord and Savior and made a commitment to helping others through his ministry." (2)

John and his friend Clay Brooks went to Mexico to work as missionaries during the 80's and early '90s. Clay was the director of the language school at the Calvary Ministerial Institute located in Nuevo Leon (near Monterey) in Mexico. (3) Apparently this is where John learned to speak Spanish also. John used his skills at fixing things (especially cars) to assist the people of this poor community. He served as a handyman as well. According to Clay, John "was a great carpenter, especially in making fine furniture… He loved his old Chevy wagon that he had restored… But most of all he loved Jesus, and helping those less fortunate…"

Ed Decker, another friend of John's, also recalls him fondly, by saying that "John was a good missionary… ministering to those around him. His skill as a mechanic kept many an old appliance, car, bus or truck running. He lived a servant's life there as he shared the Lord along with the gifts of love, humor and grace." (4)

After John returned from Mexico in the early '90s, he attended City Church in Bellevue, Washington. It was there where he was later to become employed. The church's facilities manager, Eston Catlett, remembered John well. John served in a variety of areas around the church. Over time John became friends with the church's Senior Pastor, Wendell Smith. On one occasion John accompanied Rev. Smith on a trip to Pueblo, Mexico. Pastor Wallace was the primary speaker that day at this associate church in Mexico that he visited. It was this same church in Mexico that Reverend Smith's church helped to sponsor.

I recall last seeing John during a college (football) homecoming weekend event in 1997 (over 25 years after I graduated from Linfield). I didn't really get much of a chance to talk to John too much that day. However when John heard a gospel CD I was playing in my car, he expressed to me how much he liked it. With that I was happy to give it to him. The compact disc was a fabulous compilation of gospel music by Aretha Franklin entitled *Amazing Grace*.

Little did I know that God had genuinely touched John's life a number of years earlier. From what I understand and after talking to John's long-time friend, Ed Decker, John was positively influenced by his mother's commitment to her faith in Christ. According to Ed, John had become dedicated follower of Christ prior to his missionary work in Mexico. John took on a servant's mantle. He served as a missionary in Mexico for approximately 10 years living in a very poor community in Mexico.

During the early part of 2000, John continued his close relationship with his mother. He visited her regularly and was worried about her health. (5) He was concerned about his ailing sister as well.

John decided to move into a condo on the east side of Bellevue, Washington. Though he never married, John took great pride in the close relationships he had with his nephews and sisters.

John passed away on December 27th, 2010 after a long battle with a liver disease. He died only a few hours after his mother, who also died that same day. The good news is that they are both in Heaven right now!

Due in part to his association with City Church over the years, John became friends with a number of residents in the Bellevue and Kirkland communities in Washington. Evidence of this can be seen by the many sympathetic messages from friends that were in the condolence section of the Sunset Hills Memorial Park (SHMP) and Funeral Home newsletter. Many other condolences can be viewed in the *Seattle Times* newspaper as well.

John Parrett's life was a quiet and assuming one, but it is certain that he was met in Heaven with the words, "Well done, thou good and faithful servant."

The City Church's pastor Wendell Smith died just a few weeks before John and his mother, Jean went to Heaven. The church is now named Church Home and is led by Wendell's son, Judah Smith.

For more information on the church and its staff, you can go to the website: www.churchhome.com

Caption: Four Spiritual Laws - tract (front cover of booklet)

Chapter 13

Bill Bright: His Amazing Story & Wonderful Accomplishments

B ill Bright was born in Coweta, Oklahoma on October 19, 1921. He was the son of Forest, a cattle rancher, and Mary Bright, a former teacher who had six children over the years. After Bill graduated from high school, he attended Northeastern University. In 1942 he enlisted in the United States Navy Reserve. After the war, he moved to Los Angeles where he would work in the retail candy business. It was during this time when Bill decided to attend the First Presbyterian Church in Los Angeles. The young man was encouraged to make a decision to follow Christ thanks, in large part, to Henrietta Mears who, at the time, was the Director of Christian Education for the church.

By mid-1946, Bill would decide to go to theology school (at Fuller Theological Seminary). It was also during this same year when Bill would meet his future wife, Vonette. Ultimately they became engaged but would later decide to delay their marriage due to a request by Vonette's parents. Her parents, understandably, wanted them to delay their marriage plans until after their daughter graduated from college.

They both agreed that Vonette's parents request was a reasonable one. While Vonette attended Texas State College for Women, Bill continued his studies at Fuller Seminary. On December 30th, 1948, Bill and Vonette were married.

After a few years the young seminarian decided to leave Fuller Seminary in order to pursue an evangelistic ministry with the goal of reaching out to college students with the gospel message of Christ. "A professor friend suggested 'Campus Crusade for Christ' as the name of the new ministry." (1) By the fall of 1951, the 'Campus Crusade for Christ' ministry was formerly founded on the campus of UCLA in Los Angeles by Bill and Vonette Bright.

During the early 1950s, the young married couple would also adopt two young boys (by the name of Brad and Zackary). As the Bright's ministry grew in Los Angeles, their dear friend, Henrietta Mears, helped the young evangelist and his wife by opening up her Bel Air home to the young couple.

After 18 months the Bright's ministry had demonstrated a lot of success as evidenced by the fact that over 250 students at UCLA had come to Christ in a relatively short period of time. Some of those new believers included "the student body president, the campus newspaper editor, and many athletes like Rafer Johnson who later became an Olympic gold medalist in the decathlon." (2)

It was around this time when Bill and Vonette would decide to branch out their new ministry and start more chapters in other colleges and universities around the country.

By 1958, Campus Crusade for Christ became actively involved in "launching "a work in South Korea" … due to the work and guidance provided by Dr. Joon Gon Kim. This outreach was just the beginning of a ministry today that reaches out to many countries around the "world." (3)

Bill and Vonette Bright realized the great need of 'spreading the gospel' message to these young college students around the country. By 1962 God provided enough funds for their ministry to expand their operations by purchasing a facility in Arrowhead Springs, CA.

Many who were associated with the ministry (of Campus Crusade for Christ) understood that it was during the 1960s when our country and its young population were going through a period of change. With the increased popularity of drugs like marijuana and other stimulants, it was important that these young students hear 'the good news' of God's love and the message expressed by his Son, Jesus Christ

It was also during this time when Campus Crusade for Christ would use a little booklet entitled 'Have You Heard of the Four Spiritual Laws' to reach out to millions of people including many college students as well. While Mr. Bright wrote a number of books through the decades, he is perhaps best known for his this little 15 page booklet.

The message of this little Four Spiritual Laws booklet was to clearly spell out to the public the message of salvation as found in the New Testament of the Bible. The content of this gospel presentation was created by Mr. Bright in 1957. (4) It was also during the next decade when his tract 'Have you heard of the Four Spiritual Laws' began to be distributed all over the country. The ministry used this wonderful 15 page tract to reach out to many thousands of students in colleges and cities all over the country and later, the world.

Overall this booklet supports the message of the God's love and how to find salvation with a variety of Bible verses and quotes. It begins by stating that "God loves you and offers a wonderful plan for your life". This statement in the tract is clearly supported by scripture.

It continues (on page 4 to 5) by stating that "man is sinful and separated from God. Therefore he cannot know and experience God's love and plan for his life". Again, this declaration is clearly backed up scripture. The Bible verses presented in the booklet are from the book of Romans in the New Testament: verses 3:23 and 6:23.

On page 6 & 7 we are given God's salvation plan: "Jesus is God's only provision for man's sin. Through Him you can know and experience God's love and plan for your life." This statement is backed up by Roman's 5:8 that says: "God demonstrates His own love towards us in that while we were yet sinners, Christ died for us." Page 6 also includes the Bible scripture (1 Corinthians 15:3-6) which supports the fact that Christ rose from the dead by also stating that "He appeared to more than five hundred" witnesses of His resurrection from the dead.

Additionally Christ himself declared in John 14:6 that "I am the way, and the truth, and the life: no one comes to the Father but through me."

The final section of the Four Spiritual Law's tract (pages 8 through 15) plainly and simply explains how to receive Christ into your heart by prayer. The little booklet further explains that "receiving Christ involves turning to God from self (repentance) and trusting Christ to come into our lives to forgive our sins and to make us what He wants us to be".

A simple example of a prayer where one can give our life to Christ can be read on page 10 of the booklet. Further pages of this wonderful booklet will provide a new believer with some valid suggestions on how to grow in one's faith as a new believer in Christ.

Pages 12 to 15 (of the Four Spiritual Laws) provide some valid suggestions on how one can grow in their new faith in Christ along with encouraging new believers to:

-Reading the Bible each day

-Find a Bible believing Church to attend

-Obey God (John 14:21)

-Trust God for every detail in one's life

-Allow the Holy Spirit to empower one's life

-Share the 'good news' of Christ with others

By 1967, 600 students along with a number of Campus Crusade for Christ staff members converged "on the University of California,

Berkeley for one week of confronting the hot bed of campus activism (UC, Berkeley) with the … message of the gospel. More than 700 students and faculty members received Christ" that week. (5)

In 1972 Bill Bright's ministry became involved in promoting 'Explo '72. Explo '72 was a six day event that was held in June of 1972. Besides instructing students and participants with discipleship training, the purpose of the event was to encourage believers to share the gospel with their friends and relatives.

The conference was focused on teaching discipleship training. It was attended by approximately 80,000 participants who converged at the Cotton Bowl stadium in Dallas, Texas for this gathering. The June 12th through 17th event also featured guest speakers including evangelist Billy Graham and gospel musicians like Johnny Cash and the gospel band, Love Song.

Over the years, Campus Crusade for Christ, (CCCI; now CRU) has successfully reached out to millions of college students across the country. In many cases, they have established local chapters of CCCI in over 2,000 college campuses.'(6) In addition to that, CRU has developed an extensive network of associations with thousands of Christian churches and outreach organizations worldwide.

Bill himself has authored more than 100 books and booklets. In 1979, his organization also sponsored the making of the *Jesus Film* which was further used as an evangelistic tool by Mr. Bright's organization. The film became the most translated motion picture in history resulting over time (according to www.cru.org) to millions of decisions for Christ.

Looking back, the creation of Mr. Bright's basic and clearly explained salvation message tract was a brilliant idea. In 1965 the booklet was copyrighted by Campus Crusade for Christ. Little did Mr. Bright know that our loving God would use this tract to reach millions of people around the world. Presently CRU (formerly Campus Crusade for Christ) claims that there have been over two billion Four

Spiritual Laws booklets and versions published and printed during the last 55 years.

Bill Bright died in 2003. He died at the age of 81. Bill's wife and sweetheart, Vonette, passed away on December 23, 2015. Both of them are now in Heaven and incredibly both have left an incredible evangelistic legacy which is still thriving today.

The world headquarters for CRU (formerly Campus Crusade for Christ) is now located in Orlando, Florida. You can learn more about this influential worldwide ministry by going to their website: www.CRU.org.

Epilogue

There are innumerable ways today which demonstrate how our Heavenly Father attempts to reach out to mankind with His message of salvation through His dear Son, Jesus Christ. The Lord God will use anyone who is willing to share the good news of Christ in addition to an number of other ways too.

One basic and personal way is for a follower of Christ to speak to another person about the reality of God love's for us as demonstrated in the life of a friend, a relative or even an individual you may not personally know. It is my prayer that testimonies like the ones that are in this book will touch your heart.

All I know and all I realize is that the God of Heaven and Earth loves you and wants to have a personal relationship with you. If you currently do not have a loving relationship with our Lord, I pray that you will ask Christ into your heart. I pray that you ask Him to be your Lord and Savior along with asking Him to forgive your sins.

The main purpose of Jesus coming to this world is to die for the sins of mankind. Without His incredible sacrifice: dying on the Cross, our pathway to a relationship with God would be to no effect. We must be 'born again.'

Christ defeated death and rose the third day after he was crucified on the Cross. You can now defeat sin by allowing Jesus to be your Lord and Savior. God is a loving God and He is reaching out to you and millions of people around the world with the message of

Salvation (through Jesus Christ). Just read the quote in the book of John (John 3:16)!

Thankfully, besides testimonies (like the ones in this book) there also are many other ways our loving God reaches out to millions of people around the world. God uses missionaries, numerous Christian evangelical churches, Christian radio stations, Christian television programing, internet evangelical websites, bibles (which are available in a plethora of languages), as well as Christian books, and tracts to reach out to those who need to hear the message of God's love.

If you are currently a believer and follower of Christ, I strongly encourage you to share this book with your friends and relatives (especially those who do not know our dear Lord and Savior). I also encourage you to support various ministries that strongly support reaching out to people around the world with the gospel message. It is just another way of fulfilling Christ's plea to "go into all the world and preach the gospel." (Mark 16:15)

You can be part of that in anyway God calls you to be. Whether you support this evangelical effort financially, or you personally reach out to your neighbors or friends, God delights in your efforts to fulfill His ministry of reaching out to the lost.

May the Lord bless you in this effort! God can and will use anyone to deliver His message of love and forgiveness. Even You! God Bless!

Chapter References / Endnotes

Chapter 1: Dwight (Ike) Eisenhower
(1)   Biography.com – President Eisenhower
(2)   Wikipedia.org – Dwight Eisenhower
(3)   DwightEisenhower.net – Military Career
(4)   DwightEisenhower.net – The Eisenhower Diaries
(5)   History.com – President Dwight Eisenhower
(6)   Presidentialrhetoric.com Eisenhower
(7)   ChristianityToday.com Eisenhower
(8)   WashingtonPost.com President who made B. Graham America's pastor
(9)   Theology – Eisenhower's Religion by M. Tooley (2011)

Chapter 2: Kiri Nguon
(1)   In person interview of Kiri with author (2020)
(2)   Iexplore.com history of Cambodia
(3)   Christiansunite.com/religion
(4)   Wikipedia.org politics of Cambodia

Chapter 3: Rock Hudson
(1)   Biography.com – Rock Hudson
(2)   Wikipedia.org – Rock Hudson
(3)   (2a) Wikipedia.org – Rock Hudson / the later years
(3)   Phone interview with Par Boone by the author (2021)

(4)   Phone interview with Rev. Terrance Sweeney, PHD (2021)

Chapter 4: Lawrence Hill
(1)   2020 interview by the author with Lawrence Hill includes quotes
(2)   Wikipedia.org Edwin Hawkins

Chapter 5: Gary Puckett
(1)   Phone interview with Gary Puckett by the author
(2)   Allmusic.com G. Puckett biography by Jason Ankeny
(3)   Wikipedia.org Gary Puckett and the Union Gap

Chapter 6: Prince Chapel by the Sea & the early black pioneers of La Jolla
(1)   La Jolla Light newspaper – La Jolla's Black Pioneers
(2)   La Jolla, CA Black Pioneers & Pioneer Descendants 1880-1974 / 4th ed.
(3)   La Jolla Light newspaper (religion) by Corey Levitan 12/05/18
(4)   Phone interview with Rev. Denise L. Jackson

Chapter 7: Mickey Rooney
(1)   'Life is too short' (book) by author M. Rooney (page 7)
(2)   'Life is too short' by author Mickey Rooney (page 9)
(3)   'Life is too short' by author Mickey Rooney (page 13)
(4)   'Life is too short' by author Mickey Rooney (page 20)
(5)   'Life is too short' by author Mickey Rooney (page 44)

Chapter 7 [continued]:
(6)   Life is too short' by author Mickey Rooney (page 57)
(7)   Wikipedia.org Mickey Rooney - Broadway shows
(8)   Grandtimes.com Mickey Rooney: Hollywood, Religion
(9)   Movieguide.org Stories of faith & miracles (D. Howard)
(10)   Godreports.com M. Rooney's encounter with busboy angel (M. Ellis)

Chapter 8: Linfield College during the early '70s

(1)   Wikipedia.org Linfield University – history

(2)   Email letter dated: 03-08-21 from D. Tillstrom (class of '71)

(3)   Email letter dated: 02-26-21 from Dave Lower ('Athletes in Action')

(4)   Email letter dated: 01-29-21 from Charmaine (Sanders) Klein

(5)   Linews (college newspaper), dated: 02-24-72, page 8

(6)   Email letter dated: 02-15-21 from Mike Hanna

(7)   Email letter dated: 02-05-21 from David Kuykendall

(8)   Email testimony sent 2021 from Bob Prouty

(9)   Nickolas Burt obituary Pittsburg Post-Gazette dated 10-21-05

(10)   Email letter dated 02-05-21 from Tim McGill (brief testimony)

(11)   Phone interview with Rick Loomis (2021)

(12)   The Oregonian (newspaper) May 6, 1972 'Jesus people … pg. 15

Chapter 9: Adlai Mack

(1)   Phone interview of Adlai Mack with the author – 2021

(2)   Continuation of phone interview - 2021

(3)   Quote from 2021 phone interview with Adlai Mack

(4)   Written text of manuscript corrections by Rev. Mack

Chapter 10: Ann B. Davis

(1)   Wikipedia.org Ann B. Davis (parts of chapter's 1st & 2nd pages)

(2)   Guardianlv.com 'Ann B. Davis dead at 88' by Heather Tillman

(3)   Gospellightsociety.com 'Ann B. Davis salvation through Christ'

(4)   Episcopalnewsservice.org RIP: Ann B. Davis, Brady Bunch's Alice, will be sorely missed by Pat McCaughan

Chapter 11: James Hartline

(1)   Phone interview of James Hartline with author – 2020

(2)   Continuation of phone interview – 2020 (a)

(3)   Continuation of phone interview - 2020 (b)

(4)   Continuation of phone interview - 2020 (c)

Chapter 12: John Parrott

(1)   Legacy.com John Vincent Parrott/ condolence entry: L. Anderson 05-17-13

(2)   Seattle Times newspaper (obituary) 01-19-11

(3)   Information provided by Clay Brooks

(4)   Eulogy provided by S.H.M.P. Funeral Home by Clay Brooks

(5)   Phone conversation by Eston Catlett, church facilities manager

Chapter 13: Bill Bright

(1)   Cru.org History of CRU (page 5 quote)

(2)   Cru.org History of CRU (page 6 quote)

(3)   Cru.org History of CRU (page 6 quote)

Chapter 13: Bill Bright (continued)

(4)   Information provided by CRU archives assistant

(5)   Cru.org History of CRU (page 8 quote)

(6)   Cru.org What we do (page 2)

CPSIA information can be obtained
at www.ICGtesting.com
Printed in the USA
LVHW080607060723
751621LV00016B/61